THE QUEST FOR CHARACTER

THE QUEST FOR
CHARACTER

WHAT THE STORY OF SOCRATES AND ALCIBIADES TEACHES US ABOUT OUR SEARCH FOR GOOD LEADERS

MASSIMO PIGLIUCCI

BASIC BOOKS

NEW YORK

Basic Books
Hachette Book Group
1290 Avenue of the Americas, New York, NY 10104
www.basicbooks.com

Printed in the United States of America

First Edition: September 2022

Published by Basic Books, an imprint of Perseus Books, LLC, a subsidiary of Hachette Book Group, Inc. The Basic Books name and logo is a trademark of the Hachette Book Group.

The Hachette Speakers Bureau provides a wide range of authors for speaking events. To find out more, go to www.hachettespeakersbureau.com or call (866) 376-6591.

The publisher is not responsible for websites (or their content) that are not owned by the publisher.

Print book interior design by Trish Wilkinson.

Library of Congress Cataloging-in-Publication Data

Names: Pigliucci, Massimo, 1964– author.
Title: The quest for character : what the story of Socrates and Alcibiades teaches us
    about our search for good leaders / Massimo Pigliucci.
Description: First edition. | New York, NY : Basic Books, 2022. | Includes
    bibliographical references and index.
Identifiers: LCCN 2021061886 | ISBN 9781541646971 (hardcover) |
    ISBN 9781541646957 (ebook)
Subjects: LCSH: Character. | Socrates. | Alcibiades. | Leadership.
Classification: LCC BJ1521 .P48 2022 | DDC 183/.2—dc23/eng/20220610
LC record available at https://lccn.loc.gov/2021061886

ISBNs: 9781541646971 (hardcover), 9781541646957 (ebook)

LSC-C

Printing 1, 2022

To Caley and Jennifer, who make my own quest for a better character well worth the effort.

CONTENTS

1

CAN VIRTUE BE TAUGHT?

Virtue is nothing else than right reason.
—SENECA, LETTER 66.32

CAN WE MAKE OURSELVES INTO BETTER HUMAN BEINGS? CAN we help others do the same? And can we get the leaders of our society—statesmen, generals, businesspeople—to care about the general welfare so that humanity may prosper not just economically and materially but also spiritually? These questions have been asked for over two millennia, and attempting to answer them is crucial if we want to live a better life and contribute to building a more just society.

Within the Western tradition, with which this book is concerned, the issue of becoming a better human being has often been understood in terms of "virtue." Before we can sensibly ask whether and how virtue can be taught, then, we need to discuss what exactly virtue is and why we should care about it. These days the word has acquired a rather old-fashioned connotation, as our thoughts are likely to wander toward Christian conceptions of virtues such as purity and chastity. The term has, accordingly, fallen into disuse. Google Ngram shows a pretty steady decline from 1800 on, plateauing for the past half century or so.

That's unfortunate, and it is a trend that we need to reverse, not because the old-fashioned notion is one to cling to but because an even more ancient conception still offers us much valid guidance on how to live today. The ancient Greco-Romans focused on four so-called cardinal virtues, understood as character traits, or behavioral inclinations, that ought to be cultivated and used as a moral compass to navigate our lives.

Plato is the earliest source to articulate the virtues,[1] and the Roman statesman and philosopher Cicero considered them central to the conduct of our lives.[2] They are

- Prudence (sometimes called practical wisdom), the ability to navigate complex situations in the best way possible.
- Justice, understood as acting fairly toward others and respecting them as human beings.
- Fortitude (or courage), encompassing endurance and the ability to confront our fears.
- Temperance, the ability to practice self-restraint and to act in right measure.

A modern study coauthored by psychologist Katherine Dahlsgaard and colleagues[3] found that these same cardinal virtues are near-universal across human cultures, though they are sometimes accompanied by additional valued character traits, such as a sense of human connection and a sense of transcendence. We will return to this point near the end of the book. For now, it is easy to see why the four Platonic virtues are highly regarded across traditions: a person who acts prudently, justly, courageously, and with temperance is the kind of person we often see as a role model for ourselves and our children.

While the word "virtue" comes from the Latin *virtus*, meaning specifically moral strength, the original Greek term was *arete*, which meant "that which is good" or, more succinctly, excellence. Not just moral excellence but excellence of any sort. For instance, an excellent athlete would be one who won many competitions at Olympia. And *arete* does not apply just to human beings. An excellent lioness is one skilled at catching antelopes and other prey so that she and her offspring can survive. This concept even applies to objects: an excellent knife, for example, is one characterized by a sharp blade that cuts cleanly. In general, *arete* has to do with the proper function of a thing and how well that function is carried out. The function of a knife is to cut; the function of a lioness is to produce and feed her offspring; the function of an athlete is to win competitions.

But what is the *arete* of a human being? Here opinions varied among the Greco-Romans, just as they vary today among both philosophers and scientists. But not, in either case, as much as one might imagine.

The Epicureans, for instance, thought that human beings naturally seek pleasure and, especially, avoid pain. So an excellent human life is one that is devoted to minimizing pain and maximizing pleasure.[4] For the Stoics, what distinguishes our species is the ability to reason and our high degree of sociality, from which it follows that we should spend our existence intent in using our mind to improve social living.[5] Although these conceptions appear divergent, both the Epicureans and the Stoics agreed that we should act virtuously because doing so helps us live "in accordance with nature," meaning our nature as a particular biological species.

Modern scientists such as comparative primatologist Frans de Waal[6] have also reached the conclusion that human nature is characterized by our use of reason to solve problems as well as by the unusually high degree of sociality particular to our species. Indeed, de Waal thinks that what we call morality evolved in *Homo sapiens* from preexisting building blocks found in other social primates. Morality, then, has a clear and important biological function: to regulate communal living so that individuals within a group can survive and flourish.

It is interesting to note that the modern terms "ethics" and "morality" have revealing roots in this respect: the first one comes from the Greek *êthos*, a word related to our idea of character; the second one is from the Latin *moralis*, which has to do with habits and customs. Ethics or morality, in the ancient Greco-Roman sense, then, is what we do in order to live well together—the same problem faced by our primate cousins.

In order to live a good life, we need a society where people act virtuously, a goal that was not that difficult to achieve within the small social groups that characterized much of the history of humanity and continue to mark other species of primates as well. In that sort of society, everyone knows and is likely related to everyone else. Under such circumstances, it is relatively easy to make sure that individuals act virtuously because if they don't, the other members of the group will know and will exert physical punishment or enforce ostracism on those who do not comply. Explicit ethical teachings are not necessary for the task, and both early humans and other primates could rely on their evolutionary instincts.

But human beings have not lived in small and manageable groups at least since the onset of the agricultural revolution, about ten thousand years ago. That event led to the evolution of increasingly larger stable settlements that eventually gave origin to the first cities. Those events were what ultimately triggered, in ancient Greece and Rome just as much as everywhere else on the globe, the need to develop explicit systems of ethics and related systems of laws. Simultaneously, people also began to consider whether and how they could teach the next generation to live virtuously, and especially how they might best select good leaders to handle increasingly stratified and complex societies—leaders who would act virtuously for the benefit of all.

In the West, one of the first pivotal figures to seriously explore the question of character and whether virtue can be taught was Socrates of Athens, who lived between 470 and 399 BCE, a period in which his native city, host of the first democratic government in the world, experienced its apex and fall.

In the Platonic dialogue known as the *Meno*, the title character directly asks Socrates the question that underlies the book you are reading now: "Can you tell me, Socrates, is human excellence something teachable? Or, if not teachable, is it something to be acquired by training? Or, if it cannot be acquired either by training or by teaching, does it accrue to me at birth or in some other way?"[7]

Socrates seldom answered a question directly. Instead, he would respond by asking questions of his own, aimed at guiding his interlocutors through a process of reasoning that might lead them to an answer, or at least a better understanding of the issue. Such is the case in the *Meno*.

Socrates begins by asking what virtue is, on the grounds that if we don't know the answer to that question, then we have no hope of answering the further question of whether it can be taught. Things don't go too well. Socrates informs Meno that he doesn't know what virtue is, and moreover, he claims to be unaware of anyone else who does. Meno responds that, according to one of Socrates's famous rivals, Gorgias, different people display different virtues depending on their roles in society: men in their prime are courageous, women are chaste, older people are wise, and so on. But Socrates will have none of it: virtue doesn't depend on age or sex; it is a human universal.

Despite having told Meno that he is ignorant of the nature of virtue, Socrates clearly nudges his friend in certain directions rather than others. For instance, he says that temperance and justice, two of the cardinal virtues, are found both in children and in older men, implying that they may be common to all ages. Near the end of the dialogue, Socrates considers the possibility that virtue is a kind of knowledge. If so, there should be people capable of teaching it, but Socrates doesn't see any of them around—despite the contrary claims of the likes of Gorgias and the other Sophists, a group of philosophers who commanded high fees from their students precisely because they claimed to teach virtue and who were regular opponents of Socrates in Plato's dialogues.

Often Platonic dialogues end in a state of *aporia*, a useful Greek word meaning impasse or puzzlement. This is by design because, according to Socrates, wisdom begins with admitting that we don't know what we thought we knew. Yet, in the case of the *Meno*, Socrates seems to reach a definite conclusion: virtue cannot, in fact, be taught.

If we were to stop with the *Meno*—too bad for the project of this book! However, in another Platonic dialogue, the *Protagoras*, Socrates arrives at the exact opposite opinion and determines that virtue can, after all, be taught.

Protagoras was one of the most famous Sophists. Early in the exchange, Protagoras predictably claims that Sophists can make people into better citizens by teaching them virtue. Socrates responds that while this would be very nice, it cannot actually be done because virtue is not a skill such as, say, medicine or architecture, which can both be learned by associating with someone who is good at them.[8] Socrates advances multiple arguments in favor of his thesis, but a crucial one is that it is common knowledge that virtuous parents often fail to have virtuous children.[9] He provides several examples, including that of Pericles, the charismatic statesman then in charge of Athens. His two legitimate children, Paralus and Xanthippus, were known in town for being useless and of poor character. A third, illegitimate son, Pericles the Younger, was executed in 406 BCE for unbecoming behavior after the naval battle of Arginusae during the Peloponnesian War.

Protagoras counters with several arguments in favor of the notion that virtue can be taught, one of which is particularly interesting.[10] He presents it by way of a thought experiment, a standard tool in philosophy. Imagine a town whose survival depends crucially on its citizens playing the flute. What would happen? Flute playing would be taught to everyone, both at home and in schools, regardless of age, social status, and so forth. Of course there would be some who were naturally gifted and would soon excel at flute playing. Others would turn out mediocre players, but everyone in the city would be a better player because of the education they received. That is why, says Protagoras, it is so important to teach virtue, especially to the next generation.

By the end of the dialogue, Socrates actually changes his mind and comes around to the notion that virtue can, indeed, be taught (although, interestingly, Protagoras also changes his mind on the topic as a result of Socrates's own arguments!).

So what did Socrates really think about whether virtue can be taught? It's complicated. Both the *Meno* and the *Protagoras* are often considered somewhat early dialogues, meaning they were written by Plato early in his career. The early dialogues are assumed to present positions closer to those of the real Socrates, while the middle and late dialogues use Socrates as a character to put forth Plato's own evolving ideas. But the *Meno* also contains a fascinating episode in which Socrates helps a young slave boy to demonstrate a geometrical theorem that the slave certainly couldn't have learned on his own.[11] In the dialogue Socrates claims that he is acting as a philosophical midwife, helping the boy uncover some knowledge that he already had. Where did such knowledge come from? The stunning answer we are given is that the boy learned the theorem in a previous life! This is Plato's theory of knowledge as "recollection," and it is a hallmark of mature Platonic, not Socratic, thinking. So we might tentatively conclude that the Socrates of the *Protagoras*— the one who argues that virtue can be taught—is closer to the position taken by the historical Socrates.

Be that as it may, the next leap forward in the discussion about whether virtue can be taught is made by Plato's most famous student (and Socrates's grandstudent, so to speak), Aristotle.

MORAL VS. INTELLECTUAL VIRTUE

The Watergate break-in of June 17, 1972, which eventually resulted in the resignation in disgrace of American president Richard Nixon, was a pivotal event in modern US politics. The episode was used by a former president of the University of Notre Dame, the Reverend Theodore Hesburgh, to illustrate the claim that the modern educational system in the United States fails students because it doesn't teach virtue. Hesburgh arrived at that stunning conclusion by arguing that since the men who broke in were lawyers, they were presumably educated. And yet they did something that was clearly unethical. Ergo, the educational system is to blame.

As Southwest State University's philosopher Hugh Mercer Curtler points out,[12] Hesburgh's argument is a classic example of "nonsense on stilts." For one thing, Hesburgh takes for granted a direct causal link between schooling and education, which Curtler argues is at the very least questionable. More importantly for our purposes, Hesburgh assumes a positive answer to the question we have entertained so far, apparently oblivious to a crucial complication inserted into the discussion by Aristotle.

Aristotle makes the key point in the *Nicomachean Ethics*, one of the most important books ever written on moral philosophy: "Excellence [*arete*], then, being of two kinds, intellectual and moral, intellectual excellence in the main owes both its birth and its growth to teaching (for which reason it requires experience and time), while moral excellence comes about as a result of habit, whence also its name [*ethike*, meaning moral] is one that is formed by a slight variation from the word for 'habit' [ethos]."[13] Aristotle is saying that there turn out to be two, not one, kinds of *arete*, or human excellence, pertinent to the moral sphere. One is moral excellence proper; the other he calls intellectual excellence, though the latter is also concerned with how to behave ethically.

Moral excellence, according to Aristotle, is the result of habit and repetition, though modern science would also suggest that it may have an innate, genetic component. This means that moral excellence will be broadly set early in our lives, which is why teaching it will be problematic. How early? Freud suggested that we don't change our personality much after age five or thereabouts. But as in many other things, Freud was wrong.

Modern research shows that personality traits (measured by the so-called Big Five: openness, conscientiousness, extraversion, agreeableness, and resilience) stabilize around age thirty in both men and women and regardless of ethnicity.[14] This should perhaps not be too surprising, as the human brain continues to develop, both neuroanatomically and in terms of cognitive skills, until the midtwenties.[15] The upshot is that we can be a bit more optimistic than Aristotle and Freud about being able to teach moral excellence. But how do we do it?

Think of Protagoras's example of flute playing. The sooner you start a child in musical education, the better. Such education consists of a little bit of theory and a lot of practice. That is, after all, how you get to Carnegie Hall. But even if your innate musical abilities will never make you Carnegie Hall material, you will improve with mindful (as opposed to rote, or passive) repetition. A good teacher will start you with easy exercises and then will begin to challenge you with more and more difficult ones until you can master at least a passable rendition of your favorite songs.

The same goes for moral virtue, where the obvious immediate teachers are your parents or caretakers. They will explain to you basic things about right or wrong as well as why you want to be a good rather than a nasty person. But mostly it will be practice by repetition until you internalize the habits of basic ethical behavior, such as not lying unless there is a very good reason, not taking advantage of others even if you could get away with it, and so on.

What about intellectual excellence? As we grow up, life throws more and more complex situations in our path, and it is during these challenges that developing Aristotle's second kind of excellence becomes crucial. Intellectual virtue allows us to develop practical wisdom, one of the four cardinal virtues, that is, the ability to successfully navigate life's trade-offs while maintaining our integrity as decent human beings. As Curtler puts it, while the goal of moral virtue is to set the basic framework for ethical action and the construction of our character, the goal of intellectual virtue is to refine our character, to make it capable of dealing with life as adults. Considering the example of a college course in business ethics (not an oxymoron!), Curtler says, "A course in business ethics will not make an undergraduate business major an honest employee when she goes to work after graduation. But it will sharpen her analytical skills and make her aware of the subtleties of rationalization and wary of sophistry.... [As a result of humanistic studies] we become more fully aware of the consequences of our actions, the range of our influence, and the boundaries of our world."[16]

Another way to put this is that moral virtue sets the ends toward which we work, while intellectual virtue allows us to think more carefully about those ends, and especially about the means that are most effective to reach them. When Seneca, the first-century Stoic philosopher and adviser to the emperor Nero, wrote the words with which this chapter begins, "Virtue is nothing else than right reason," he meant reason deployed to achieve the right ends, that is, a combination of moral and intellectual virtue.

WHAT THIS IS ALL ABOUT

The book you are reading is an exploration of some famous successes and failures in teaching others, and ourselves, about virtue. The overall goal is to answer the questions I posed at the beginning of this chapter: Can we make ourselves into better human beings? Can we help others do the same? And can we get the leaders of our society to care about the general welfare so that humanity may prosper not just economically and materially but also spiritually?

Most of the examples that we will examine are drawn from larger-than-life figures of the ancient Greco-Roman world because those cultures paid particular attention to both the theory and practice of living virtuously and left us ample documentation of their worries. We will encounter the likes of Socrates and his friend and student Alcibiades, whose unvirtuous behavior had a lot to do with the fall of his city, Athens, by the end of the Peloponnesian War. We will follow the courageous attempts of Plato, Socrates's student, to teach virtue to two tyrants of the Sicilian city of Syracuse—which almost cost him his life. Our quest will then bring us to consider the relationship between Aristotle and Alexander the Great as well as that between Seneca and Nero.

We will take seriously the argument that only people who are already predisposed to virtue can further refine it and live accordingly by studying examples such as Cato the Younger, the archenemy of Julius Caesar and a practitioner of Stoic philosophy; the emperor-philosopher Marcus Aurelius, who relied on his Stoicism in order to deal with two frontier wars, a rebellion, and the worst plague to strike the ancient world; and Julian of Constantinople, forever known as "the Apostate" because he dared counter the rising Christian tide by using the resources of his chosen philosophy, Neoplatonism. These were all leaders of their generation: emperors, conquerors, kings, and generals. We will look at their efforts from the point of view both of statesmanship and of moral philosophy.

Naturally we will then turn to the broader question of what, exactly, the relationship between politics and philosophy ought to be, starting with the mother of all treatises in political philosophy, Plato's *Republic*; continuing with the radical contribution of Machiavelli; and ending by considering some modern takes on the issue.

Finally we will land, safely or not, back in our own era and consider what developing virtue and character might mean for people like you and me. We are unlikely to have a chance to mentor the next Alexander or Nero (not that the world needs more of that sort of individual anyway!). And we are also not likely to become generals or high-level politicians ourselves. But we do have plenty of chances to influence other people—be they our children, partners, friends, students, or colleagues. And, of course, we have a chance, and arguably a duty, to work on ourselves, to try to become at least slightly better human beings than we were yesterday. How do we do this? Near the end of the book, we'll draw on the lessons learned during our quest, as well as on research in contemporary social and moral psychology, to see what may or may not work.

Most people don't think twice about spending a significant amount of effort and resources to get ahead in their career, or even just to maintain their physical health as long as they can. But when it comes to our character—what the ancient Greco-Romans thought is our most precious possession—we hardly give it a thought. And yet, there is an art to living, and that art can be learned by doing practical philosophy, which means critically reflecting on our own life experiences as well as the experiences of others, with the intention of learning how we can do better. Day by day, year after year. The second-century Stoic philosopher Epictetus admonished his students, "Most of us dread the deadening of the body and will do anything to avoid it. About the deadening of the soul, however, we don't care one iota."[17]

We should care. Let's begin to learn how.

2

ALAS, ALCIBIADES, WHAT A CONDITION YOU SUFFER FROM!

Then alas, Alcibiades, what a condition you suffer from! I hesitate to name it, but, since we two are alone, it must be said. You are wedded to stupidity, best of men, of the most extreme sort, as the argument accuses you and you accuse yourself. So this is why you are leaping into the affairs of the city before you have been educated.

—PLATO, *ALCIBIADES I*

KNOW THYSELF, OR FORGET ABOUT POLITICS

The first example of a concerted attempt at teaching virtue that we will examine—in some detail, since it's a great story in this regard—is that of Socrates and his friend, student, and rumored lover Alcibiades. Which is a bit ironic since we've just seen that Socrates may or may not have thought that virtue can be taught in the first place. The year is 430 BCE. The place, Athens. The time, shortly after the beginning of the Peloponnesian War between Athens and Sparta, which—twenty-six years later—will end in Athens's defeat and a general weakening of the Greek city-states, so much so that they will soon become easy prey, first of Philip II of Macedon and then of his son Alexander "the Great."

But that will come later. Right now, two friends are in the midst of a momentous conversation that will mark not just their lives but the future of the city they love: Socrates and Alcibiades, the philosopher and the future statesman and general. Socrates is about forty years old, while his companion has just turned twenty. Despite his youth and inexperience, or more likely because of it, Alcibiades is full of self-confidence. He tells Socrates that he doesn't need anyone or anything. He can rely on his own strengths, from his undisputed physical beauty to his penchant for daring, from his noble ancestry to his considerable wealth.

The young man is preparing to appear, a few days later, in front of the Athenian people. He is looking forward to the occasion, which he fully believes will result in honors being showered on him the likes of which have never been granted before, not even to his adoptive father, the statesman Pericles—who will die the following year, struck by the plague that has already put Athens at a great disadvantage in its war against Sparta. A war, incidentally, that has been orchestrated in part by Pericles himself.

Socrates throws cold water on Alcibiades's expectations. He warns Alcibiades that he will not accomplish the things he wants to accomplish without Socrates's help. That's bold talk! But Socrates backs it up with an observation to which his young companion readily assents: Sound advice about politics and statesmanship comes from those who actually know and have thought about such things, not from wealth, which is Alcibiades's main asset. I hardly have to point out the relevance of this remark to us denizens of the twenty-first century, two and a half millennia after Socrates spoke.

The philosopher underscores his point in his usual way, by analogy. Suppose you wish to give advice on food, explaining to people that a particular foodstuff is better than another one and that it should be consumed in this quantity. Then someone stops you and says, "Wait a minute, what do you mean 'better'?" And your response is "I mean more healthy, of course!" But it turns out that you are not, in fact, a doctor, and you know nothing about health. Surely that would be disgraceful, though that hasn't stopped ancient and modern charlatans alike.

The ongoing conversation isn't about food and health; it's about the just way to conduct the business of the state. Socrates, accordingly, asks Alcibiades how he managed, as a mere child, to distinguish between what is just and what is unjust. The young man immediately acknowledges that, well, as it turns out, he didn't really discover the difference between justice and injustice all by himself. Instead, he learned it, just like everyone else. But Socrates is far from satisfied: Be more specific, my friend. Learned from whom? From the many, comes the response. Although Socrates does not have the tools of contemporary logic at his disposal and can't name Alcibiades's logical fallacy as we would today (vox populi, to be precise), he knows it when he sees it: Learning from the multitude is no guarantee of learning anything of value. Just as you would want a doctor, not the people at large, to diagnose your illness and prescribe your medicine, you shouldn't attempt to govern a nation on the basis of popular opinion.

Contemporary commentators often refer to Socrates's attitude as probing and humorous. Probing it certainly was, with Socrates being the self-appointed gadfly of Athens. But his sense of humor more often than not bordered on sarcasm and frequently plainly crossed that border. Sure enough, the philosopher now addresses Alcibiades as "the beautiful," the son of Cleinias, and one who does not understand what is just and what is unjust, yet pretends to understand and has the gall to advise the Athenian people about it! He really ought to refrain from such behavior because "it is a mad undertaking you intend to take in hand, best of men, to teach what you do not know, having taken no care to learn it."[1]

Having set the tone and shown Alcibiades that he is actually ignorant of the things he thought he knew, Socrates attempts to teach his young pupil. The dialogue is a splendid example of the so-called Socratic method, often referred to as *elenchus*, Greek for cross-examination.

First, approach someone who thinks he is wise and knowledgeable and ask him questions—often rooted in pertinent analogies—aimed at uncovering whether he really is wise and knowledgeable. Usually the fellow turns out to be anything but.

Second, if your interlocutor agrees that he doesn't actually understand the matter at hand, begin to teach him—again often deploying analogies—by way of a series of suggestions. Once the other has agreed to the first suggestion, use it as the starting point for a chain of reasoning that ends with the conclusion that you wished to arrive at to begin with.

Third, either establish the point or—more frequently—secure the other person's assent and then immediately proceed, by the same method as above, to show that, upon further consideration, even the initial, tentative conclusion isn't really quite sound. The inquiry needs to resume after all.

Fourth, repeat.

This is why so often (but not always!) the Socratic dialogues end in *aporia*, which doesn't sound like much of an outcome. Consider, though, that Plato tells us that the Oracle at Delphi declared that Socrates was the wisest of men. Surprised, Socrates begins questioning people who profess to be wise, seeking to prove the Oracle wrong. The more he questions, however, the more he discovers that the alleged wise men are actually self-important and deluded fools. It finally dawns on Socrates that what the Oracle must have meant was that he is wisest in the minimalist sense that at least he realizes that he is ignorant. It is no surprise, then, that many of his conversations end without settling the issue.

However, Xenophon, in his *Apologia*, recounts a tellingly slightly different story: "Once on a time when Chaerephon made inquiry at the Delphic oracle concerning me [Socrates], in the presence of many people Apollo answered that no man was more free than I, or more just, or more prudent."[2] Which makes sense of the fact that—indirectly, at least—often Socrates knows exactly where his interlocutors are going wrong and, more importantly, where they should aim if they wish to go right. His conversation with Alcibiades is one such case. Let's rejoin it.

Socrates now mounts an argument that arrives at the preliminary conclusion that what we discover to be admirable is also good from a moral perspective. Alcibiades readily agrees. And, continues the philosopher, good things are also advantageous things. That's right, comes the reply. Ah, but the two of them have previously agreed that if something is just, it is also, necessarily, admirable. Only a minute ago, they also agreed that what is admirable is good and that good things are advantageous, all of which implies that what is just is also advantageous. Here is how the argument works, schematically:

Premise 1: If something is just, it is necessarily admirable;
Premise 2: If something is admirable, it is also good;

Premise 3: Good things are advantageous, so
Conclusion: If something is just, it is also advantageous.

Pause for a moment and realize that this is a stunning conclusion, not just for that time and place but for all times and places. A common misconception is that what is just is often at odds with what is advantageous. For instance, it may be advantageous for me to take a larger share than my guests of the food at the dinner table, but it isn't just. Likewise, it may be advantageous for a politician to allow himself to be bribed, but it isn't just. And so on.

Socrates's notion here is that—when we look at things properly—there simply is no difference between what is just and what is advantageous. Why? Because what everyone wants is to be a good person, and a good person is a just one. So it is to everyone's advantage to be just. But I'm getting a bit ahead of myself.

Socrates resumes his probing of Alcibiades by trying a different approach. He asks whether Alcibiades is ever confused about the number of his eyes. Is he sure he has only two eyes and not three? What about the number of his hands? Two or four? Alcibiades at this point is so doubtful of his own convictions that he is afraid to answer even such obvious questions, but he eventually admits that no, he is never unsure about the number of his eyes or hands. That, Socrates continues, is because Alcibiades actually knows the answers to those questions. By contrast, when Alcibiades gives first one answer and then another about what Athens's priorities should be, that's a sure indication that he has no knowledge to be dispensed but only very tentative and often changeable opinions. People are confused about what they don't know, not about what they have mastered.

There are three possibilities at play. Someone has knowledge about whatever subject matter is under discussion, or they don't have knowledge but are aware of their ignorance, or they don't have knowledge and are unaware of their ignorance. Those with the first two types of knowledge are not likely to make mistakes, either because they actually know what they are talking about or because they are aware of their limitations. It is the third group that is likely to make mistakes, and in this scene, Alcibiades belongs to this last unfortunate class. This condition of ignorance is, Socrates claims, a contemptible type of stupidity. Socrates goes on to frankly berate not just Alcibiades but most members of the political class: "Then alas, Alcibiades, what a condition you suffer from! I hesitate to name it, but, since we two are alone, it must be said. You are wedded to stupidity, best of men, of the most extreme sort, as the argument accuses you and you accuse yourself. So this is why you are leaping into the affairs of the city before you have been educated. You are not the only one to suffer from this; most of those who manage the affairs of the city are the same way, except a few—perhaps including your guardian, Pericles."[3]

This, then, according to Socrates, is the real problem with many politicians: They are fools, affected by a particular kind of ignorance—arguably best referred to as unwisdom—yet blinded by their own unwavering conviction that they actually know what they are doing. There are few exceptions, and Pericles, Alcibiades's adoptive father, *perhaps* counts as one. As we can again easily appreciate, not much has changed in the intervening twenty-five centuries.

Alcibiades is understandably dejected but—resourceful as he is—immediately comes up with an excuse for himself. He points out to Socrates that his mentor would be right if the other politicians had actually prepared well for their job. In that case, he would be like an athlete, having to train hard in order to be able to compete at the Olympics. But politicians, Alcibiades continues, are not like athletes. They just show up for the job and rely on their charisma in order to convince people to go along—then as now, we may add. Therefore, argues Alcibiades, he doesn't need to worry, as his natural gifts, including his unquestionable good looks, will surely and easily beat the competition.

Socrates is not convinced. Indeed, he berates Alcibiades again—such an "excellent man" (note the Socratic sarcasm here) who has just said things unworthy of his looks, not to mention his other advantages! Stunningly for the culture of the time, Socrates now invokes the authority of a woman to further his argument. The woman in question is the Persian queen Amestris (a name that, incidentally, means "strong woman"), the wife of King Xerxes and the mother of his successor, Artaxerxes, whom Alcibiades fancies he will be able to take on one day on behalf of the Greeks.

Socrates's invocation of Amestris is surprising not just because she is a woman but also because she certainly didn't have a good reputation among the Greeks. For instance, Herodotus has this to say about her: "I am informed that Amestris, the wife of Xerxes, when she had grown old, made return for her own life to the god who is said to be beneath the earth by burying twice seven children of Persians who were men of renown."[4] It's likely that, on this occasion at least, Herodotus was not well informed at all but rather highly biased, as the Greeks had an understandable antipathy for the Persians, who more than once attempted to conquer them.

Be that as it may, Socrates imagines Amestris wondering aloud about Alcibiades's ambitions. What sort of foundation is he basing them on? Surely nothing but care and wisdom, the only qualities of worth that the Greeks happen to be known for. But then she learns that Alcibiades has barely turned twenty, that he is entirely uneducated, and that, moreover, he refuses to listen to Socrates, the very person who loves him and is in a position to advise and train him. The youth is content with the way he is and fancies that his qualities are enough to enable him to take on the Great King! And what do his qualities consist of? Beauty, physical height, family, wealth, and his wits. Amestris would conclude, Socrates claims, that Alcibiades must be mad!

According to Socrates, Alcibiades needs to take to heart the inscription at Delphi: *Gnothi seauton* (know thyself). If he does, he will realize that the very things he considers to be his assets—beauty, height, family, wealth, and wits—are actually his worst enemies. And one more thing will hamper Alcibiades throughout his life: his boundless ambition. While most people, even today, think of ambition as a good thing, Socrates suggests that it leads us to do things for the wrong reasons: not because they are just, honorable, and good but only in pursuit of self-aggrandizement.

Maybe, just maybe, not all is yet lost for Alcibiades. He seems to grasp, at least in part, what Socrates is telling him. He admits that he has long been living in a disgraceful fashion without even realizing it. Socrates tells him to take heart. Had he realized this by the time he was fifty, he would have been too late. But he is young; he can still change his ways and embrace the path of wisdom. And he has Socrates, his teacher, who loves him.

What are we to think of Socrates's claim that he loves Alcibiades? Much has been made of their relationship, including the more or less overt implication that they were lovers in the physical sense of the term. This, I hasten to say, would not have been unlikely or frowned upon. Indeed, such a relationship was known as pederasty, a word that at the time did not have the horrible moral implications that it has today. Pederasty in ancient Greece was a well-recognized relationship between an elder (male) person, the *erastes*, and a younger male, usually in his teens, referred to as the *eromenos*. The notion was that the *eromenos* would learn about life—and not just in the sexual sense—from his mentor, the *erastes*. The relationship was not supposed to linger much past the *eromenos*'s teenaged years, and it shouldn't be confused with our modern conception of homosexuality, though the latter was also recognized, at least in certain parts of Greece. Perhaps the most spectacular example is the famous Sacred Band of Thebes, an elite group of soldiers made up of 150 male couples who were instrumental in ending the Spartan domination of their city.

We actually know from Alcibiades's own words, as spoken in Plato's *Symposium* and to which I will turn later in this chapter, that Socrates and Alcibiades did not engage in an *erastes-eromenos* type of relationship. To Alcibiades's chagrin, it must be added.

Still, Socrates does love Alcibiades in the way that a philosopher loves his pupil. And he appeals to the pupil by pointing out that people who profess to love Alcibiades's body do not ipso facto love Alcibiades himself. Moreover, those are the people who will leave as soon as Alcibiades's body begins to age and lose its beauty, as is bound to happen. However, the person who really loves you, because he loves your soul, will stick with you through thick and thin—so long, warns Socrates, as the soul itself keeps getting better, that is, so long as Alcibiades maintains a course of ethical self-improvement, the philosophical art of living.

Socrates, then, truly loves Alcibiades, while other people love only what temporarily belongs to Alcibiades. That something is already beginning to fade, even as Alcibiades himself, as a human being, is just on the verge of blooming. The danger is that Alcibiades will let himself be corrupted, and his soul turn ugly, by becoming a lover of the people, that is, a lover of adulation, fame, and glory. In order to avoid this fate, Alcibiades must take the precaution that Socrates recommends: First learn what he needs to know to successfully manage the affairs of Athens and only *then* actually put forth his candidacy for such an important public role. Proceed in this order, Socrates advises Alcibiades, and nothing terrible will happen to you or the city of Athens.

Now, if one wishes to manage the affairs of the state in a good and admirable fashion, one must offer excellence to its citizens. And excellence—meaning *arete*, excellence of character, or virtue, as we have seen in Chapter 1—is something that Alcibiades does not yet have, and cannot possibly yet have, because it is acquired by way of mindful experience: not just the passage of time and the accumulation of practical knowledge but also the habit of critically reflecting on one's experiences and learning from them. One doesn't become wiser just because one grows older.

Such excellence of character, Socrates tells Alcibiades, implies that a person is concerned not just with what belongs to him but also with what belongs to the entire community. Being a good leader has little to do with power or authority; rather, it has to do with moderation and justice. Ignoring this and instead acting unethically for one's own advantage, or even for the perceived advantage of the city, would be to act in ignorance of what is good both for oneself and for one's community, in direct defiance of the Oracle's injunction.

Alcibiades is moved by Socrates's loving and wise words, and he resolves then and there to abandon his earlier ways and care for justice only. But Socrates is not optimistic. Intuiting the dark fate that awaits Alcibiades and Athens, in addition to his own end, Socrates replies, "I'd like you to keep on doing that. But I am filled with dread, not because I do not trust in your nature, but because I see the force of the city and fear that it will overcome both me and you."[5]

The lure of the dark side is ever strong.

BE CAREFUL WHAT YOU PRAY FOR

Some time later, Socrates and Alcibiades meet again, and on this occasion, the conversation hinges on what one should properly pray for as well as on the foolishness of human beings. Again we see Socrates attempting to keep Alcibiades on the path of the philosopher, instructing him before he embarks on his political career in order for that career not to turn out to be ruinous for both Alcibiades and Athens.

Alcibiades is on his way to pray to a god, though we are not told what god it may be. This could be on purpose. While most Athenians believed, or professed to believe, in the Olympian pantheon, Socrates seemed to have a conception of a single god and in fact asks Alcibiades whether he is going to pray "to *the* god." It is in part for this reason that Socrates will eventually be tried on charges of impiety, which is not atheism but rather belief in gods different from those officially worshipped in the city.

The philosopher immediately steers the conversation toward the subject of foolishness, inducing his pupil to agree that most people are fools, though there are different degrees of the condition. Some are foolish in the highest degree, and we call them mad. Others—affected to a lesser extent by the malady—are just naive, silly, or stupid. In fact, Socrates maintains, there are many different kinds of foolishness, just as there are many different kinds of artistry or disease. Someone may be a painter, a sculptor, or a musician, yet all of these are artists. Some people may be struck by the plague, the gout, or tuberculosis, yet we properly say that they are all sick. And it's not just that these things come in different kinds; they also come in different degrees, precisely as foolishness does. Someone may be a better or worse painter, sculptor, or musician, and plague, gout, and tuberculosis may strike some more than others.

An interesting example of a fool, continues Socrates, is Oedipus, the mythical king of Thebes. The story is well known to us because of three famous tragedies by Sophocles: *Oedipus Rex*, *Oedipus at Colonus*, and *Antigone*. Oedipus travels to the sacred site of Delphi, where the Oracle—the same one who declared Socrates to be the wisest man in all of Greece—tells Oedipus that he is fated to kill his father and marry his mother.

Wishing to avoid this ghastly future at all costs, Oedipus leaves the city where he grew up, Corinth, as well as his father, King Polybus, and his mother, Queen Merope. He heads for Thebes, where he is determined to build a new life for himself. On his way there, however, he meets and quarrels with an old man and ends up killing him. Oedipus will discover later that the man in question was none other than King Laius of Thebes, his real father, who had ordered the infant Oedipus to be killed precisely to avoid the outcome predicted by the prophecy.

What happened was that the man in charge of leaving little Oedipus exposed to the elements on a mountainside, a shepherd and servant of Laius, had pity on the infant and instead passed him on to another shepherd. The second shepherd brought

Oedipus to Polybus and Merope, who adopted him as their own son. Oedipus, therefore, has grown up with foster parents in a foreign city without being aware of it.

When Oedipus arrives in Thebes, he finds the city terrorized by the Sphinx. Our hero challenges the monster, attempting to answer the famous riddles in order to free his newly acquired fellow citizens.

> "Which creature has one voice and yet becomes four-footed and two-footed and three-footed?"
>
> "Man—who crawls on all fours as a baby, then walks on two feet as an adult, and then uses a walking stick in old age."

The Sphinx is flabbergasted by the cunning of a mere mortal but poses a second riddle:

> "There are two sisters: One gives birth to the other, and she, in turn, gives birth to the first. Who are the two sisters?"
>
> "Day and night."

(In Greek, both words are declined in the feminine.) Humiliated again, the Sphinx throws herself from a high rock and dies. The reward for Oedipus's bravery is the hand of the recently widowed queen, Jocasta, who of course we know actually is Oedipus's mother.

A few years pass, and Thebes is struck by a plague. Oedipus inquires about the reasons for such divine punishment and in the process discovers that he has killed the king, his father. Jocasta, realizing that she has married her son, hangs herself. When he sees this, Oedipus picks up two of the pins from the queen's dress and uses them to blind himself.

The story is about the role individuals play in the unfolding of cosmic events as well as about flawed human nature. But the reference to the Oracle at Delphi and the fact that Oedipus ends up blinding himself are particularly telling: The protagonist of the myth fails to see what is in front of his eyes, and the reason for that, ultimately, is that he has not embraced the Delphic injunction: Know thyself.

Socrates mentions Oedipus because he wants to remind Alcibiades that one ought to be wary of what one hopes, and especially prays, for. He then presents a series of scenarios to his young friend. Suppose, Socrates says, that the god you are about to pray to all of a sudden appears before you and grants you the power to become the tyrant of Athens. (Being a "tyrant" in ancient Greece did not have the negative connotations that the word acquired later. It simply meant absolute ruler.) But perhaps that wouldn't be such a big deal for Alcibiades. Then maybe the god could make him the tyrant of all of Greece. And if that were still not enough, the god could grant him all of Europe. Would Alcibiades like that? So prompted, the youth answers that not only he but pretty much anyone else would be pleased if such a thing happened.

Socrates retorts, "That's precisely the problem!" Many strive to become tyrants because they think they can do better than others, only to end in disgrace or even death. Most wouldn't refuse this power and even pray to become tyrants or generals or to take on other powerful roles that, once actually obtained, have the potential to do more harm than good. Some of those people eventually change their tune and actively pray to be rid of the very things that they so foolishly desired.

Alcibiades mulls over all of this and agrees that not knowing what is good is very dangerous. Indeed, ignorance harms not only the person who lacks such knowledge but also many others who will be affected by that person's foolish actions. Why, then, do so many people act on the basis of their ignorance of what is truly good or bad?

Indeed, the sort of knowledge Socrates is talking about is a prerequisite for the correct use of any other kind of knowledge. Consider people who have some kind of specialized expertise but have no grasp of what is good or bad—what we usually refer to as wisdom. They may know, for instance, how to build walls or maintain harbors. But they don't know why they should, or should not, do so. Or take those who have the skills necessary to conduct wars but not to determine whether a given war is just or unjust.

Socrates then prepares himself for the rhetorical kill. He reminds Alcibiades that he previously agreed that most people are foolish and very few are sensible. Moreover, their discussion has established that when people act on the basis of what they think they know, more likely than not they will end up hurting themselves because in reality, they don't have the understanding that is necessary to act well in life. When Alcibiades nods his agreement, Socrates turns his attention to his friend's own ambition and warns him, "So too it is necessary that one remove the mist from your soul, the mist that is there now, and only then apply that through which you are going to recognize both bad and good alike. You don't seem to me to be able to do this now."[6]

It turns out that Alcibiades will never be able to do it, right up to the end of his life.

ON THE NATURE OF LOVE

A number of years have passed. It is 416 BCE, Socrates is fifty-four years old, and Alcibiades is a man in his full powers at age thirty-four. The place, again, is Athens, specifically the house of the poet Agathon. Two nights earlier, he won the first prize for tragedy at the festival of Lenaia, held in January.

As was often the custom, the winner is hosting a symposium—literally a drinking party—with some of his friends. Normally these events feature rather heavy drinking and a lot of singing, but Agathon has opted for a more intimate celebration, asking his close friends to take turns offering a speech in praise of love.

That single word, nowadays, is used to indicate a number of different sentiments, from love of our children to love of country to romantic love. The modern idea of romantic love, in particular, probably traces back to the medieval concept of chivalry, a notion made popular by French, Italian, and Spanish troubadours and finally canonized for Western audiences during the Romantic era that followed as a backlash against the Enlightenment.

The ancient Greeks had a more nuanced view of love, recognizing four partially overlapping forms of it, none of which actually corresponds to our conception of romantic love.

To begin with, there is *agápē*, which means love with an aspect of charity, in the sense of benevolence, embedded in it. This is the sort of love that we have for our children and for our spouse or partner. Early Christians adopted the term to mean the unconditional love of God for his children. As Thomas Aquinas put it, *agápē* means "to will the good of another."[7]

Second is *érōs*, which in part does mean, as the modern word "erotic" indicates, sexual attraction. However, as we shall see in a moment, Plato expanded the concept to indicate, after an individual matures and contemplates things properly, love for beauty itself. This is the origin of the phrase "Platonic love," which does not necessarily mean love without sex but rather love of the ideal form of Beauty, which may begin with erotic attraction but eventually transcends it.

Third is *philía*, which describes a sense of affection and regard among equals. Aristotle uses this word to characterize love between friends, for family members, or for community. It is a virtuous type of love of a brotherly sort with a component of enjoyment.

Last is the less frequently used *storgē*, meaning affection, especially (but not only) of the kind one has toward parents and children and including empathy of the type felt naturally toward one's children. *Storgē* is also used to indicate love for one's country or even for a sports team and—interestingly—situations in which one must put up with unpleasant things, as in the oxymoronic phrase "love for a tyrant."

Note that what distinguishes the four types of love recognized by the Greeks is not so much the object of love but rather the modality of the sentiment. Take the specific instance of a long-term "romantic" relationship in the modern sense of the term. Ideally, what one wants in that case is a particular combination of the first three modes: We unconditionally (i.e., not because it is to our advantage) want the good of the other person (*agápē*); we want not just physical attraction but also a deeper appreciation of the beauty of our partner in terms of his or her character traits (*érōs*); and we want to be that person's friend and to enjoy his or her company for its own sake (*philía*). What distinguishes love for a partner from love for our children, friends, country, or God, then, is the specific modulation of the various types of Greek "love."

One of the most beautiful passages in the *Symposium* is the speech given by the comic poet Aristophanes. Seven years before the party at Agathon's house, Aristophanes—rather unsuccessfully—produced *The Clouds*, a comedy of ideas, as we would call it today, in which he lampooned several prominent Athenians, including Socrates. Plato did not take kindly to Aristophanes's representation of his mentor—whom Aristophanes confused with a Sophist, Socrates's perennial target of criticism. Later, Plato actually partially blamed the poet for the negative verdict at the trial that led to Socrates's death. Aristophanes's treatment of Socrates, however, did not stop the latter from attending the symposium or Plato from presenting Aristophanes as a brilliant character in his own dialogue.

At the symposium, Aristophanes tells Agathon's friends the mythical tale of how *érōs* originated. You see, the original human beings were complex creatures with four arms, four legs, two faces, and a rotund body. They went around doing cartwheels and were very powerful. There were three types of original humans: males, females, and what Plato calls "androgynous," half male and half female.

One day, humans decided to take on the gods and started to scale Mount Olympus. Zeus initially simply wanted to obliterate them with his signature thunderbolts but then thought better of it, as he wished to keep enjoying their worship of him. So instead he used his thunderbolts to cut each human in half and scatter the halves across the world.

It is for this reason that we constantly long for our soulmate, *the* half that we lost during our misguided assault on the gods. When a female half meets her female counterpart, we have a lesbian relationship; when a male half meets the corresponding male half, we have a male homosexual relationship; and when a female and a male half rejoin, this results in a heterosexual relationship. Aristophanes tells us that homosexuals are the bravest and most manly of all human beings, as is evidenced by the fact that they typically become politicians. By contrast, heterosexuals are unfaithful and adulterous, not to be trusted. Whether this observation about politicians is made sarcastically or literally is not clear, though I lean toward sarcasm.

The myth is meant to explain the otherwise puzzling feeling of blessedness we experience when we meet our soulmate, because he or she literally *is* our lost half. It is a beautiful story, though Aristophanes arguably meant it as a satire of the very popular origin myths then circulating among the Greeks and certainly not as a factual account. In the *Symposium*, Aristophanes ends the story with a warning: We had better curb our hubris, or Zeus may cut us down again, and this time, we'll be condemned to hop around on a single leg!

The last speech of the symposium is given by Socrates himself. It begins in typical Socratic fashion, by way of back-and-forth questioning with the host, Agathon. But then, rather uncharacteristically, Socrates launches into an actual speech of his own, telling the other guests how he was instructed on love by Diotima of Mantinea—one of the few cases of an ancient philosopher mentioning a woman as his mentor, though this is the second instance we encounter of a woman teaching Socrates!

Diotima recounted another myth of the origin of love to Socrates. The gods were celebrating the birth of Aphrodite. One of the guests was Plutus, the god of health, who got drunk and fell asleep. A bit later, a mortal named Poverty arrived at the party to beg from the gods. She saw Plutus passed out and decided to sleep with him, becoming pregnant with Love.

As a result, Love is not a god but a daemon, a term that for the Greeks had a neutral meaning, not the decidedly negative one later imposed on it by Christianity. Love is a creature halfway between gods and mortals. Love inherited his mortal mother's ugliness and also his father's godlike knowledge of beauty and ability to pursue it. In this story, Love is born halfway between ignorance and wisdom and constantly tries to overcome the first in pursuit of the second. Love is, in a sense, a philosopher, a word that literally means a lover and pursuer of wisdom.

Diotima then told Socrates, as he recounts to Agathon's guests, that men vary in their nature. Some devote themselves to the pursuit of love of the body, while others pursue love for both body and mind. The first kind of man is really no different from other animals, always seeking pleasure and material goods; the second kind of man, however, is interested in wisdom and virtue. From there, Diotima instructs Socrates in how the pursuit of love evolves in a worthy man (in ancient Greece, women were unfortunately left out of the picture, even in this story told by a woman). Such a worthy man should at first love a specific body, that of a person he finds beautiful; next, he should expand his appreciation to all human bodies; then, he should graduate to loving beautiful minds and finally to loving the idea of Beauty itself.

At this very moment, an inebriated Alcibiades crashes the party and ends up giving a speech, not in honor of the idea of love but in praise of his only real flesh-and-blood love: Socrates.

Alcibiades is initially surprised to find Socrates at the banquet and even accuses him of always lurking in places where Alcibiades does not expect to see him. Socrates protests to the host, Agathon, that he needs someone to defend him from Alcibiades, "for my love for this man is no light matter." Socrates says that ever since he laid eyes on Alcibiades, he has never been able to look at anyone else, no matter how beautiful they may be. But on his part, Alcibiades—mad as he is made by his affection for his mentor—has envied and abused Socrates. Moreover, Socrates charges, Alcibiades can't help but lay hands on him. Socrates asks Agathon to intercede to reconcile him with Alcibiades, or at the very least to defend him if Alcibiades should attempt to use force.

What is going on here? As the dialogue makes clear immediately after this dramatic exchange, Socrates's love for Alcibiades is of a very different nature from the love that Alcibiades harbors for Socrates. The philosopher loves the virtue of his pupil, or at least the potential for virtue. Alcibiades, by contrast, wants physical intimacy with his mentor. They both speak of *érōs*, but they are clearly in pursuit of two very different aspects of it.

"But there's no reconciling me and you," replies Alcibiades, adding that he will be revenged on Socrates for spurning his love at some other time. While saying this, Alcibiades arises and takes a garland. On this night, he says, Socrates deserves a garland because, unlike the playwright Agathon—who by means of his words won a transient honor at the theater festival a couple of days before—Socrates wins whenever he speaks. With these words, Alcibiades lays the garland on Socrates's head.

At this point, one of the other guests, Eryximachus, intervenes. He is a physician who will be indicted the following year—together with Alcibiades—in a famous scandal involving the profanation of sacred images. In the *Symposium*, Eryximachus explains the rules of the evening to the late arrival, Alcibiades, inviting him to participate, as everyone else has done so far, by giving a speech in praise of love.

Alcibiades accepts the challenge and begins his speech, not in praise of love but in praise of Socrates, a speech that takes a bit of an odd form. First, Alcibiades says that Socrates is like the satyr Marsyas. This is a doubly interesting choice, for Marsyas—like all satyrs—is famously ugly. And so is Socrates, something he himself occasionally made fun of. But, more importantly, Marsyas is a mythical example of hubris, as he dared to challenge the god Apollo in a musical contest. The satyr, predictably, lost the contest and with it his life. Plato here might be hinting at the notion that Socrates challenged Athens itself and lost his life as a result, just as Marsyas did.

Alcibiades says that Socrates is like the statuettes of the satyrs one can find in Athenian shops, ugly on the outside but containing an image of the gods inside. Not even Socrates, continues Alcibiades, disputes that he is indeed ugly. But the similarity with the satyr does not stop here. You see, Socrates—like Marsyas—is affected by hubris, and Alcibiades can provide witnesses to that effect should the charge be denied by his mentor. Despite his physical ugliness and his hubris, though, Socrates has the power to enchant everyone who listens to him. In fact, says Alcibiades, people are transfixed by Socrates's words even when they are repeated by someone else who doesn't come close to the rhetorical power of the philosopher: "Whether a woman hears it or a grown man or a young man, we are all stunned and possessed."[8]

Relevant to our focus here, at this point Alcibiades's speech becomes revealing of the speaker's own inner turmoil. He declares that Socrates has often made him feel something no one else has been able to manage: shame. This shame comes from the fact that when he is with Socrates and listens to his arguments, Alcibiades agrees that he should not care for anything but virtue. And yet, as soon as he leaves Socrates's side, he slides back into yearning for the fame and glory that can be bestowed upon him by the multitudes. This conflict is so acute that Alcibiades admits that on many occasions, he has wished Socrates dead. And yet, as soon as the thought takes form, he also immediately knows that if Socrates actually were to die, he would feel miserable. "So I just don't know what to do with this man."[9]

Then again, says Alcibiades, Socrates is simply not concerned at all by whether someone is handsome. In fact, he is full of contempt not just for physical beauty but also for wealth and all the other things that most people care about. These things are the very source of happiness to many, but to Socrates, they are utterly worthless. According to Alcibiades, Socrates finds more value in spending "his whole life being ironic and joking with people."[10]

We are then treated to Alcibiades's account of how he has repeatedly tried and failed to seduce Socrates. First, he managed to be alone with him, hoping that he would hear from Socrates's lips the sort of things that lovers long for. He was disappointed. Socrates talked about the usual things he talked about with everyone, such as the nature of piety or justice. And at the end of the day, he simply went away. Undeterred, Alcibiades invited Socrates to exercise with him, and the philosopher agreed. This time, Alcibiades thought, we'll get somewhere. They went to the gymnasium, and Socrates wrestled with the (much younger) Alcibiades and with no one else. But that too didn't get Alcibiades where he really wanted to go. At some point, Alcibiades even managed to spend the night with Socrates in his own house. But again, nothing came of it: "When I got up I'd slept the night with Socrates no differently than if I had slept with my father or an older brother."[11]

Why is Alcibiades so hopelessly attracted to Socrates, whom he has just described as being as ugly as a satyr? Because Alcibiades fell in love with Socrates's words, which struck at his heart, his soul, or wherever the words of a philosopher hit their target. These words take hold of someone in a fiercer fashion than a serpent, comments Alcibiades, fastening on a young soul and prompting the person so struck to do or say anything.

He then turns to Socrates and makes a direct plea: You are the only one worthy of my love, even though you seem hesitant to return my affection. I will give you anything that is my property and grant you any favor you ask because I recognize that—as you say—nothing is more honorable than to become as good as I can be, and nobody can help me more on this path to goodness and virtue than you, Socrates.

This strange mix of reproach, contempt, and praise continues during what we might nowadays characterize as Alcibiades's stream of consciousness in front of Agathon's friends. He tells Socrates that it is a well-known fact that the mind becomes sharper as the eyesight begins to fade, though Socrates himself is certainly not old when the action takes place. Indeed, Alcibiades reminds the others attending the symposium, Socrates has repeatedly shown more endurance in war than Alcibiades himself, not to mention everyone else in the army. On those occasions when they were cut off from their provisioning lines and had to go without food for a while, Socrates was the one most able to endure the situation. And when there was feasting and drinking, Socrates could outdo everyone in that department as well, without ever getting drunk!

Once, during a military campaign, Socrates stood without motion from dawn to evening, apparently mulling over some philosophical point. The other soldiers even brought out their bedding—as it was a cool summer evening—to keep an eye on him and see how long he would stand there. He remained in the same position through the night, and when the sun was rising, he prayed to the star and went about his business as if such behavior were normal.

Moreover, admits Alcibiades, in a famous battle after which he was honored with a medal for bravery, it was actually Socrates who, unwilling to leave his wounded friend, saved Alcibiades's life along with their weapons. And as for Socrates's way of talking, at a superficial glance, he says the same things to everyone—from cobblers to tanners to bronzesmiths—so that unreflective people laugh at his words. But if one pays attention, explains Alcibiades, the words uttered by Socrates are the only ones spoken in Athens, and perhaps all of Greece, that have any intelligence. They are divine words, describing excellence of character and nudging people to do what is good and admirable.

The company is now tired and more than a little drunk, so Alcibiades and the others head home. But Socrates, after having partaken of the wine all night long, simply gets up and walks toward the agora—the central marketplace in Athens. Unaffected by the previous evening's talk or drink, he spends his day as usual, talking to young Athenians about the nature of justice and such things.

Who, exactly, were Alcibiades and Socrates? Larger-than-life figures for sure. One a dashing, rich, and brilliant man who eventually led Athens to disaster. The other arguably the most famous philosopher of all time, who chose death at the hands of his fellow citizens rather than renounce his principles. To really appreciate their relationship, as well as why Socrates tried—and failed—to steer Alcibiades on the path of virtue, we need to take a closer look at their lives and times. We will start with Alcibiades, who made a show of his strong will and single-mindedness even as a child. These traits accompanied him until the day he died.

3

A STRONG-MINDED CHILD

He was naturally a man of many strong passions, the mightiest
of which were the love of rivalry and the love of preeminence.

—PLUTARCH, *LIFE OF ALCIBIADES*, 2.1

AN ENVIABLE START

One day in Athens a very young Alcibiades was playing with
astragali, sheep knucklebones that children would throw with
the goal of achieving the highest possible score, depending on
the exact configuration in which the bones landed. On this particular occasion, Alcibiades had just thrown the astragali, and
he must have gotten a high score. However, the bones ended up
in the middle of the street, and suddenly a wagon appeared. Alcibiades ordered the driver to stop, but the man, in no mood to
listen to a mere boy, kept going. To the terrified astonishment
of both his friends and the driver, Alcibiades jumped in front
of the wagon and dared the driver to continue. He did not, and
Alcibiades was able to retrieve the knucklebones. Plutarch, who
tells this story, fails to satisfy our curiosity about the final score
of the game, but we get a very good idea of just how determined
Alcibiades was, even as a young boy, to get what he wanted.

Alcibiades was born into one of Athens's most prominent families, the Alcmaeonidae, who claimed descent from none other than the mythological figure of Nestor, one of the characters in Homer's *Iliad*. Such good luck was tempered, however, by the fact that the Alcmaeonidae were, according to popular lore, a cursed lineage. The origin of the family curse dated back to 632 BCE. The first member of the clan, Megacles, successfully warded off an attempted coup in Athens perpetrated by Cylon and should properly have been regarded as a savior of his country. However, after securing Cylon's defeat, Megacles made the mistake of pursuing the rebels into the temple of Athena, where they had sought refuge. Megacles and his comrades slaughtered the traitors inside the temple, thus desecrating the ground dedicated to the deity protecting the city of Athens.

As a result of this desecration, the Alcmaeonidae were exiled, and the corpses of buried members of the family were exhumed and removed from within the city limits. They were allowed back in by 594 BCE, and their successive history continues to be fascinating. For one, the family was responsible for building the sanctuary of the Oracle at Delphi, which became the most prominent and influential in ancient Greece. One of the Alcmaeonidae was Hippocrates, whose daughter, Agariste, eventually became the mother of the statesman Pericles. Hippocrates's brother, Cleisthenes, overthrew Hippias, the last tyrant of Athens, and introduced the reforms that gave birth to Athenian democracy.

In an episode that anticipates Alcibiades's own tactics, Cleisthenes bribed the Oracle at Delphi to convince the Spartans to help him, which they did, albeit reluctantly. Moreover, during the Persian Wars of the fifth century BCE, the Alcmaeonidae attempted to forge an alliance between Athens and the Persian empire, just as Alcibiades would later try to do, despite the fact that Athens was actually prominently involved in the Greek resistance against the Persians. As far as we know, the Alcmaeonidae line came to an end with Alcibiades, as the family disappeared from the Athenian historical record.

But let us return to our hero. In a second childhood episode, Alcibiades was wrestling another boy, and things were not going well. Undaunted, Alcibiades bit his opponent, a rather unorthodox move, to say the least. When he was accused of fighting like a girl, he replied that on the contrary, he was fighting like a lion. He was not just determined to win at all costs but had already developed the ability to rationalize his own actions in order to deflect criticism and turn it into a point in his favor.

Stories of the young child give way to stories of the young man who was always determined to have his way. The tale of his marriage offers one example. One day he assaulted a man named Hipponicus, a wealthy citizen with an excellent reputation. Alcibiades did it just because he had made a bet with some friends who dared him. There was no other reason. No quarrel between the two, no anger between the families. Alcibiades simply walked up to Hipponicus and hit him with his fist. The fact became widely known and turned into a scandal, threatening to tarnish young Alcibiades's reputation. So one morning he presented himself at the house of Hipponicus. Once admitted, Alcibiades took off his cloak and invited Hipponicus to punish him as he thought appropriate. But Hipponicus was not the kind of man to take revenge, so he instead forgave Alcibiades and, shortly thereafter, even gave him his daughter, Hipparete, in marriage.

Hipponicus's son, Callias, negotiated a dowry of ten talents, a more-than-respectable sum at the time. Alcibiades accepted, but when Hipparete became pregnant, he went back to Callias and asked for ten more talents, declaring that that was what they had agreed to should there be children. Apparently Callias had made no such agreement, and Alcibiades simply sought to financially exploit the birth of his child.

Hipparete turned out to be a good wife who was affectionate to her husband. But Alcibiades did not repay her in kind, frequenting a number of courtesans, both foreign and local. At some point, Hipparete must have had enough, so she left the house and went to live with Callias, perhaps hoping to trigger a shift in behavior in her husband. If that was her goal, it didn't work, as Alcibiades continued exactly as before. At that point, Hipparete decided to go to a magistrate to ask for a divorce, one of the few rights accorded to women under ancient Athenian law. However, in order to file for divorce, she had to appear in person. When Alcibiades found out about her intentions, he intercepted her, seized her, and carried her home in a very public and humiliating manner, making a point of passing through the agora, the crowded marketplace in the center of town. Nobody dared to stop him or to intercede on her behalf. She was therefore forced to stay with Alcibiades and died shortly thereafter of unknown causes while he was on a trip to Ephesus.

As a prelude to his entrance into public life, Alcibiades participated in the Olympic Games. He was well known for his beautiful horses, and since he could afford it, he fielded three chariots, which had never been done before by any other city, let alone a private citizen. He was manifestly behaving like a king. Of course his chariots did well, placing first, second, and third (or fourth, according to an alternate account by Thucydides). The win was so spectacular that the famous tragedian and poet Euripides wrote an ode about it:

Thee will I sing, O child of Cleinias;

    A fair thing is victory, but fairest is what no other Hellene has achieved,

    To run first, and second, and third in the contest of racing-chariots,

    And to come off unwearied, and, wreathed with the olive of Zeus,

    To furnish theme for herald's proclamation.[1]

But even this episode of triumph was marred by Alcibiades's questionable ethics. The story goes that an Athenian named Diomedes, who was a friend of Alcibiades, was also keen on winning at Olympia. He found out that there was a racing chariot in Argos that belonged to the city but could be purchased. He asked Alcibiades to buy it for him since Alcibiades had both the means and the local contacts necessary to pull off the transaction. Alcibiades did buy the chariot on behalf of his friend but then turned around and entered it into the games as his own, bidding Diomedes—as Plutarch puts it—"go hang."[2]

Plutarch also shares a rare episode of Alcibiades's kindness, when he chose a mistress from among the prisoners from Melos and accepted the son she bore him into his household. But this story too is thrown into a darker light by a crucial and far less honorable piece of background information: It had been Alcibiades who had insisted that all the men from Melos should be put to death and the women sold into slavery.

Why was such a character so popular in Athens? Here is how Plutarch explains it: "His voluntary contributions of money, his support of public exhibitions, his unsurpassed munificence towards the city, the glory of his ancestry, the power of his eloquence, the comeliness and vigor of his person, together with his experience and prowess in war, made the Athenians lenient and tolerant towards everything else; they were forever giving the mildest of names to his transgressions, calling them the product of youthful spirits and ambition."[3]

THE GREAT WAR

Alcibiades's extravagant and somewhat mischievous behavior was well known, and well tolerated, in Athens. Had his life come down to a series of episodes such as those described so far, there would have been little point in making him one of the chief characters of this book. But his life took a very different turn—indeed, a bewildering *series* of turns—when it came to how he behaved just before and during the Peloponnesian War, the great conflict that defined his and Socrates's generation. It was also during the war that Socrates's warnings about Alcibiades's character proved to be prescient.

To understand Alcibiades's—and Socrates's—role in the Peloponnesian War, we need to first set the stage for the conflict itself. The reasons for the war went back to the aftermath of the Persian Wars that saw Athens and Sparta successfully leading the Greeks against the Persian invaders. What followed the Greek success was a period that the historian Thucydides refers to as the *pentecontaetia*, meaning fifty years, during which Athens consolidated its influence in the region, becoming a de facto empire. Its satellite states would pay regular monetary tribute that was housed on the island of Delos, officially with the aim of financing any further defensive military action against the Persians. Yet the Delian treasure increasingly became diverted to fund not just the Athenian fleet but even public works in Athens itself. It is not by chance that this period is referred to as the Athenian golden age. It was also, however, a period of increased friction with the Peloponnesian states, especially Sparta.

The situation came to a head in 459 BCE. Corinth and Megara, both Spartan allies, entered into a conflict, and Athens managed to ally itself with Megara, which would have given the Athenians an important foothold on the strategically crucial Isthmus of Corinth. Needless to say, neither the Spartans nor the Corinthians would stand for that, and the hostilities quickly devolved into what is often referred to as the First Peloponnesian War, to distinguish it from the Great Peloponnesian War that followed it. The First War lasted fifteen years and ended in a stalemate subsequent to a massive land invasion of Attica—where Athens was located—by Sparta. Greece was now a bipolar region: Gone was the famed Hellenic League, headed jointly by Sparta and Athens, that had defeated the Persians. The geopolitical scenario now pitted the Delian League under the leadership of Athens in Attica against the Peloponnesian League under the influence of Sparta. The Thirty Years' Peace signed between the two leagues in the winter of 446–445 BCE did not last half that time.

Thucydides tells us that one of various episodes that triggered the resumption of hostilities was the matter of Potidaea, a former colony of Corinth that had become a tributary of Athens. The Potidaeans were apparently none too happy about having to pay tribute, so much so that the Athenians at some point grew tired of the Potidaeans' insubordination and ordered them to tear down their defensive walls and to expel the resident Corinthian magistrates. In response, Corinth promised military support to Potidaea if it finally rebelled against Athens. This was a clear violation of the Thirty Years' Peace.

The resulting Battle of Potidaea of 432 BCE is important to our narrative because both Socrates and Alcibiades fought in it and were in fact the protagonists of a remarkable episode. At this time, Socrates was thirty-eight years old, while Alcibiades was just eighteen. At Potidaea, the Athenians faced a combined force of locals, Corinthians, Spartans, and Macedonians under Perdiccas, who was a former ally of Athens but had turned against the city. The Athenians won the day, but their success turned out to be a Pyrrhic victory. The Potidaeans did not surrender after their loss on the battlefield and instead entrenched themselves inside their city walls. The Athenians then began to lay a siege, which lasted until 430–429 BCE and cost Athens up to one thousand talents per year, a huge sum.

We have various reports of what Socrates and Alcibiades did at Potidaea, from Plato's *Symposium* and *Charmides*, Diogenes Laertius's *Lives and Opinions of the Eminent Philosophers*, and Plutarch's *Lives*. This is how Plutarch describes the events:

> While still a stripling, [Alcibiades] served as a soldier in the campaign of Potidaea, and had Socrates for his tent-mate and comrade in action. A fierce battle took place, wherein both of them distinguished themselves; but when Alcibiades fell wounded, it was Socrates who stood over him and defended him, and with the most conspicuous bravery saved him, armor and all. The prize of valor fell to Socrates, of course, on the justest calculation; but the generals, owing to the high position of Alcibiades, were manifestly anxious to give him the glory of it. Socrates, therefore, wishing to increase his pupil's honorable ambitions, led all the rest in bearing witness to his bravery, and in begging that the crown and the suit of armor be given to him.[4]

The episode tells us something important about both Socrates's and Alcibiades's characters. Socrates showed incredible courage in battle as well as loyalty to his friend, who was in great difficulty. In the aftermath of the battle, he also acted in accordance with his philosophy: External things, such as medals and praise, are simply not important. What is important is to do the right thing. Alcibiades, by contrast—while also certainly brave in battle—just as clearly showed that his priorities were precisely the reverse of those of his mentor. He craved recognition and praise, even at the cost of taking it away from his own friend and savior, who obviously deserved it far more. These contrasting patterns would mark the entire lives of the two men.

Eight years later, in 424 BCE, when the Peloponnesian War had been raging for a while and after Athens had been struck by a plague that had killed its leader, Pericles, Socrates and Alcibiades again took to the field and found themselves at Delium in the middle of the bloodiest battle of the war to that point. There, the Athenians had fortified a sanctuary of Apollo—a sacrilegious act by the recognized standards of all Greek cities—in order to establish a military presence in the enemy territory of Boeotia. The Thebans, allied with the Spartans, attacked with an overwhelming force. Armed with an ingenious machine capable of throwing flames, they quickly threw the Athenians into disarray and forced them to retreat.

In the midst of the ensuing chaos, Socrates again displayed steadfastness and bravery, as described by his young friend Alcibiades:

It was worthwhile to behold Socrates when the army retreated in flight from Delium; for I happened to be there on horseback and he was a hoplite [infantryman armed with spear and shield]. The soldiers were then in rout, and while he and [General] Laches were retreating together, I came upon them by chance.... I had an even finer opportunity to observe Socrates there than I had had at Potidaea.... Walking there just as he does here in Athens, stalking like a pelican, his eyes darting from side to side, quietly on the lookout for friends and foes, he made it plain to everyone even at a great distance that if one touches this real man, he will defend himself vigorously.[5]

Here we have another glimpse of Socrates as soldier, acting calmly and decisively in the middle of a chaotic and dangerous situation. He also participated in a further crucial battle of the Peloponnesian War two years later at Amphipolis, in 422 BCE. He was forty-eight years old by then, but Diogenes Laertius tells us that "he took care to exercise his body and kept in good condition."[6] A healthy body in a healthy mind, as the saying goes.

The battle of Amphipolis was so hard on both sides that it drained the will to fight in Athens as well as in Sparta. The two superpowers therefore signed the Peace of Nicias, named after the Athenian general who brokered it. As Thucydides remarks, it was a peace more in name than in fact, as both parties—and their allies—remained restless and constantly endangered the agreement. One Athenian in particular actively tried to undermine the peace: our friend Alcibiades, who was becoming the new rising star of the hawk party in Athens and acted in a way that gives us further insight into his character and the lack of virtue Socrates was so worried about.

Alcibiades wanted to end the Peace of Nicias, probably in great part because he was ambitious and there was no better place than the battlefield for a young man to prove his worth and further increase his prestige. According to Thucydides, who knew him personally, Alcibiades's pride had also been wounded by the Spartan decision to negotiate with Nicias, even though it was Alcibiades's family that had been the *proxeni*, that is, diplomatic representatives, of Athens in Lacedaemon. Since Alcibiades was still relatively young and inexperienced, while Nicias was an established general, this is a good indication of the oversized ego of our protagonist.

Alcibiades saw that one way to thrust a wedge into the peace accord was for Athens to form an alliance with Argos, which had the interesting double feature of being a democracy—and thus more naturally inclined toward Athens than Sparta—and of being located in the Peloponnese—and thus in a position to directly challenge Spartan hegemony. On his own initiative, since he had no official powers in Athens, Alcibiades sent a message to the Argives, asking them to dispatch representatives to Athens as soon as possible and at the same time suggesting that they should work hard on an alliance with the similarly minded cities of Mantinea and Elis.

Alcibiades's message alerted the Argives to a new warming up of the conflict between Athens and Sparta, and convinced them to turn away from ongoing negotiations with Sparta and seek an alliance with Athens instead. The three cities (Argos, Mantinea, and Elis) promptly sent a joint embassy to Athens. The Lacedaemonians countered with an embassy of their own, as they were now afraid of the potential consequences of a new alliance between Athens and Argos.

The Spartan envoys made reasonable proposals to the Athenian council, specifying that they had come with full powers of negotiation. This alarmed Alcibiades: If the Spartans were to make the same proposals and reassurances to the full Athenian popular assembly, the alliance with Argos would likely be rejected. Here is where we have a full display of the cunning and at the same time the duplicity of Alcibiades. He approached the Spartan envoys, proposing that he would use his influence in the assembly to broker a compromise favorable to Sparta on condition that the Spartans did not reveal to the full assembly what they had just told the council: that they had full diplomatic powers. His actual goal was to discredit the Spartans before the assembly and to alienate them from Nicias, who was still regarded as the chief Athenian negotiator.

The Spartan envoys fell for the trick. When they were asked in front of the assembly whether they had come with full powers, they replied that they hadn't, which directly contradicted what they had previously told the council. Alcibiades publicly revealed the contradiction, accusing the Lacedaemonians of being untrustworthy. The people of Athens at this point were ready to vote for an alliance with Argos, but the vote was postponed because of an earthquake. No major action, diplomatic or otherwise, was taken in case of natural disasters so that there would be time for the priests to interpret the meaning of the event.

Nicias too fell for Alcibiades's trick and could not understand why the Spartans had reneged on their word. Even so, when the assembly resumed deliberation, he still argued that it was not in the interest of Athens to renew the war and that the Argives should be kept at bay until they had clarified their intentions with regard to Sparta. Nicias obtained permission to go to Sparta as part of a diplomatic mission to see whether Athens could get enough concessions from its former enemy to help keep the peace that he himself had brokered just a few years earlier. The mission failed because of Spartan intransigence, and

Nicias returned to Athens empty-handed. This infuriated his fellow citizens, and Alcibiades predictably took advantage of the situation, decidedly shifting things in favor of the alliance with Argos. In the end, the attempt failed, and in part as a result of Alcibiades's trickery, full hostilities resumed. And Socrates's former pupil was far from being done. Indeed, he was just getting started.

THE SICILIAN DISASTER

Alcibiades was determined to continue the Athenian war and his major role in it. Apparently affected by no remorse for his political maneuvering that had undermined the Peace of Nicias, he now turned his eyes toward an even bigger prize: Sicily. The excuse for Athens to send a large expeditionary force to the island was that some of the Ionian cities there had requested Athenian support against the dominance of Syracuse, which, like Lacedaemon, was of Dorian ethnicity. Thucydides, however, was not fooled for a moment about the real motivations of his compatriots from Alcibiades down: "Such was the great island on which the Athenians were determined to make war. They virtuously professed that they were going to assist their own kinsmen and their newly-acquired allies, but the simple truth was that they aspired to the empire of Sicily."[7]

If conquered, Sicily would have supplied Athens with vast additional resources, beginning with grains and continuing with men and ships from the Ionian allies and the Dorian subjects. The decision to invade was made, and in 415 BCE, Athens geared up for the daring enterprise. Three commanders with full powers were appointed for the occasion: Alcibiades, Nicias, and Lamachus, the son of Xenophanes. Nicias was appointed against his will and actually warned his fellow citizens that they were embarking on the effort on the basis of flimsy excuses and without the necessary preparation. He directly and harshly (yet correctly) attacked his co-commander, Alcibiades, accusing him of acting not in the best interest of the state but only in the pursuit of self-aggrandizement. Alcibiades, with no self-irony, responded by parading his vanity: "In consequence of the distinguished manner in which I represented the state at Olympia, the other Hellenes formed an idea of our power which even exceeded the reality, although they had previously imagined that we were exhausted by war. I sent into the lists seven chariots—no other private man ever did the like; I was victor, and also won the second and fourth prize; and I ordered everything in a style worthy of my victory."[8]

Thucydides presents us with a sober analysis of Alcibiades's motives, and it is not a flattering one. Alcibiades was a natural political enemy of Nicias, but most of all, he badly wanted to command the expedition. He dreamed of conquering not just Sicily but also Carthage—which at the time had a foothold in Sicily and which later became one of the first great rivals of another rising Mediterranean power, Rome. He was certainly after glory but also after money. The sort of extravagant expenditure that he brazenly mentioned in his response to Nicias put a serious dent in his resources, large as they were. His constant quest for exotic pleasures and his maniacal need to compete in sporting events and make sure that he vanquished any competitor all cost significant amounts of money. War conquest was the surest way to replenish his coffers.

Despite Alcibiades's astounding popularity, it is interesting to note that at least three prominent people, according to Plutarch, were opposed to the Sicilian expedition. One, of course, was Nicias. A second was a certain Meton, an astrologer who presumably saw what he interpreted as an unfavorable celestial alignment. This, in turn, may have influenced Nicias, since we know that he was rather superstitious. The third person is the most pertinent to our story: Socrates. Plutarch does not provide any details about why Socrates was skeptical of the attack on Syracuse, saying only that it is likely that "he got an inkling of the future from the divine guide who was his familiar."[9]

The divine guide in question was Socrates's famous daimon, rendered in Latin as "daemon." Because of the Christian tradition, we think of demons as evil creatures, but that was not the understanding in ancient Greece and Rome. Rather, a daimon was conceived as either a lesser deity or the spirit of men from the Golden Age. If one paid attention, one could receive counsel from one's daimon, and Socrates often said that he did have a daimon and that the counsel he received most often from his spirit guide was "No," as in "Don't do it." It's doubtful that Socrates literally thought he had a direct line of communication with a divinity. The Presocratic philosopher Heraclitus had already said that a daimon is really a person's character. Invoking a daimon, then, might simply have been a metaphorical way for Socrates to refer to the path he had set for himself of never doing anything that could imperil his moral integrity. Nevertheless, as we shall soon see, one of the reasons that he was brought before the court that eventually condemned him to death was a charge of impiety, or believing in gods other than those officially recognized in Athens. The well-known story of the daimon did not help his case.

Despite the opposition of his teacher, Alcibiades ultimately carried the day in the assembly. The majority of the people were positively enthusiastic about the idea of a Sicilian expedition, and the skeptical minority was afraid to speak out for fear of being labeled unpatriotic—something that should sound familiar to twenty-first-century audiences. But at the height of the preparations, just when Alcibiades's scheming seemed to be guaranteeing the desired outcome, something strange and disturbing happened. One night, the Hermae were mutilated throughout the city.

The Hermae were square stone figures carved in the ancient Athenian fashion, explains Thucydides, disseminated everywhere, situated at the entrances of temples as well as private homes. On that fateful night, someone went around systematically disfiguring the faces of the Hermae, a sacrilegious act that shocked the Athenians and that required immediate investigation and punishment of the culprits. Moreover, there was a rumor that a group of young and arrogant aristocrats had performed the sacred rites of the Eleusinian Mysteries—normally celebrated every year as part of the cult of Demeter and Persephone—in their private homes as a game.

We do not know whether Alcibiades and some of his friends were in fact responsible for these sacrilegious acts, perhaps at the end of yet another night of excessive drinking, or whether someone else did it as part of a plot to undermine the young commander. Some suspected a group of Spartan sympathizers. We do know that a plot of some sort was afoot against Alcibiades, though. Once accused, he demanded an immediate trial so that the episode would not interfere with the imminent departure of the Sicilian expedition. But his request was not granted, and he was allowed to sail for Sicily while the charges were pending. This may have been done at the behest of his political enemies, who thus bought themselves more time to prepare their prosecution and to undermine public confidence in Alcibiades.

Notwithstanding the incident of the Hermae, the ambitious Athenian expedition to Sicily began with great hopes, and only a minority of people worried about the hubris of it all. The Athenian fleet sailed for Sicily and was welcomed in the port of Catana, north of its major objective, Syracuse.

Trouble, however, began almost immediately: In Catana, the Athenians found the ship *Salaminia*, which had been sent from home to retrieve Alcibiades, relieve him of command, and bring him to Athens for trial. But Alcibiades was prepared. Fearing an unfair trial, he managed to escape with some of his comrades to Thurii, in modern Calabria, on the Italian mainland. From there, he crossed the Ionic Sea and landed in Peloponnesus. Plutarch notes that someone recognized Alcibiades when he sneaked out to avoid capture and asked him, "Can you not trust your country, Alcibiades?" The response was "In all else, but in the matter of life I wouldn't trust even my own mother not to mistake a black for a white ballot when she cast her vote."[10] Shortly thereafter, he was made aware of having been condemned to death, to which news his comment was "I'll show them, that I'm alive."[11] He was now a fugitive and was condemned to death in absentia. In a matter of days, he had gone from hero to traitor.

As a matter of fact, he had begun to do damage to his former city before he was even apprehended. The Athenians had set up a scheme to gain possession of the important city of Messenè, on the northeastern tip of Sicily, by making contact with someone on the inside who would betray his fellow citizens and open the gates to the Athenian army—a standard way, at the time, to gain new territory without bloodshed. Alcibiades was of course aware of the Athenian plot, and before escaping, he alerted the Syracusan representatives in Messenè. As a result,

Messenè was not captured, and the Spartans—who supported Syracuse—now owed one to Alcibiades.

This series of events led to a spectacle that few would have foreseen just months earlier: the simultaneous appearance in the Lacedaemonian assembly of emissaries from Corinth and Syracuse, there to discuss the ongoing war, and the lone figure of Alcibiades, a fugitive from Athens come to make his case for why Sparta should welcome him.

In the first place, Alcibiades had to explain why someone from a democratic polis would help an oligarchic one such as Sparta. To this, Alcibiades claimed to be a democrat, not in the sense that he favored the rule of the people but in the (much) broader sense that he and his family had always opposed tyranny. An oligarchy, technically not being a tyranny, would therefore have fit his conveniently broadened conception of democracy. Second, Alcibiades exaggerated to the Spartans and their allies the scope of the Athenian plan, presenting what had been his own secret ambitions as if they were the stated intentions of his former fellow citizens, namely, to conquer first Syracuse and then the entirety of Sicily, to move against Carthage, and finally to bring the might of all of Hellas to bear against the Peloponnesians. This calamity could be avoided only, he argued, if Sparta were to lend concrete aid to the imperiled Syracusans, failing which the survival of Sparta itself would soon be in doubt.

Furthermore—and this was a crucial suggestion that would significantly alter the trajectory of the war—Alcibiades advised the Spartans to occupy and fortify Decelea. This was only two hundred stadia (i.e., about fourteen miles) from Athens, a place from which one could see both Athens itself and the ships entering its port, Piraeus. Decelea was at the crossroads of important trade routes, and controlling it would not only be a huge blow to the morale of the Athenians but would also make it much more difficult for them to receive supplies and to move freely within Attica. The advice was accepted, resulting in endless difficulties for Athens from that moment on. Finally, Alcibiades gave the following masterful piece of rationalization to explain his betrayal of the city where he had been born and that had nurtured him:

> An exile I am indeed; I have lost an ungrateful country, but I have not lost the power of doing you service, if you will listen to me. The true enemies of my country are not those who, like you, have injured her in open war, but those who have compelled her friends to become her enemies. I love Athens, not in so far as I am wronged by her, but in so far as I once enjoyed the privileges of a citizen. The country which I am attacking is no longer mine, but a lost country which I am seeking to regain. He is the true patriot, not who, when unjustly exiled, abstains from attacking his country, but who in the warmth of his affection seeks to recover her without regard to the means.[12]

Alcibiades had certainly developed a curious conception of what it means to be a patriot.

DEATH IN PHRYGIA

The Sicilian expedition eventually ended in complete disaster for the Athenians. Both their army and their navy were annihilated by the joint Syracusan and Spartan forces, and Nicias lost his life while attempting to retreat toward more friendly territory. When news of the disaster reached Athens, the people at first did not believe it. It was simply inconceivable that such a great expedition had failed so miserably. Once they accepted the truth, though, the people were angry with the leaders and orators who had promoted it—as if, observes Thucydides, the people themselves had not enthusiastically voted in favor of the assault against Syracuse.

Meanwhile, the Spartan control of Decelea, following Alcibiades's treacherous advice, was proving highly damaging to Athens's interests. Spartan helots liberated the mind-boggling number of twenty thousand Athenian slaves from the nearby silver mines, thus dealing a severe blow to the financial basis of the Athenian empire. Athens was forced to increase the tributes from its allies, which predictably led to a series of revolts that were encouraged by the Lacedaemonians. Soon it began to look as if Athens were at the end of its rope.

Alcibiades, once again, played no minor destructive role in all this. He personally made the rounds of the Ionian cities to foment their revolt against Athens, succeeding in detaching the crucial city of Chios from the Delian League. He went so far as to lead the Chian troops, now hostile to Athens. He then stopped at Miletus, where he had friends in high positions, and convinced the Milesians to join the Spartan effort. The Spartans themselves sought to widen their coalition and made a crucial alliance with the Persians, in the person of the satrap Tissaphernes, serving under King Darius II. In fact, Alcibiades fought on the side of the Milesians under Tissaphernes against the Athenian contingent sent to quell the rebellion.

But the twentieth year of the war, as chronicled by Thucydides, brought yet another unexpected plot twist: Alcibiades fell under increasing suspicion at Sparta, and there was considerable pressure for him to be put to death. What had happened? He had seduced King Agis's wife, Timaea, and impregnated her. She gave birth to a son, Leotychides, and did not even attempt to conceal his paternity. So now Alcibiades was on the run again. He certainly couldn't go back to Athens, where he had been condemned to death, so he headed for the only other option available: none other than the Persian satrap Tissaphernes. As he had done before with the Spartans, Alcibiades proved perfectly capable of giving valuable advice to his new protector, this time against both Sparta and Athens:

> Let the dominion [i.e., Hellas] only remain divided, and then, whichever of the two rivals [Sparta or Athens] was troublesome, the [Persian] King might always use the other against him. But if one defeated the other and became supreme on both elements [i.e., land and sea], who would help Tissaphernes to overthrow the conqueror? He would have to take the field in person and fight, which he might not like, at great risk and expense. The danger would be easily averted at a fraction of the cost, and at no risk to himself, if he wore out the Hellenes in internal strife.[13]

According to Thucydides, Alcibiades's real motive was not to help the Persians but rather to find a way back to Athens. Bizarre as this may sound, Thucydides has a point. Alcibiades sent a message to the Athenian contingent on the island of Samos, a state that had recently become a democracy after having killed two hundred aristocrats and thrown out the previous oligarchic government. The soldiers there knew that Alcibiades had Tissaphernes's ear and realized just how important that might be to their cause. Alcibiades promised to broker Persian help so long as the "villainous democracy" that had sent him into exile would be overthrown. Accordingly, a plan was soon hatched on Samos to undo the democratic government in Athens.

Stunningly, despite some initial resistance, Alcibiades's emissaries in Athens managed to convince the Athenian people that only Alcibiades could deliver them Persian support and that such support was predicated on a "wiser" government than the one now in charge. The Athenians decided that a delegation should be sent to negotiate with Tissaphernes and Alcibiades.

But events took an unexpected turn when a group of young supporters of Alcibiades assassinated one of the leaders of the democratic government in Athens, triggering a sudden change whereby the one-hundred-year-old democracy turned overnight into an oligarchy, the so-called rule of the Four Hundred from the number of aristocrats sitting in the new city council. The coup succeeded on June 9, 411 BCE. But the new oligarchy was immediately undermined by the fact that a second, coordinated coup in Samos failed. The Athenian navy was stationed at Samos and remained loyal to the democracy, leaving the government of the Four Hundred without a fleet. The sailors and soldiers stationed at Samos soundly rejected the legitimacy of the rule of the Four Hundred, declaring that it wasn't they who were rebelling against their city but the other way around. They deposed the generals in charge at Samos, elected new ones, and—irony of ironies—recalled Alcibiades and declared him their leader in the effort to reestablish democracy in their home city. So now Athens was governed by an oligarchy at home but had to contend with a prodemocracy navy abroad. And Alcibiades, true to character, had been instrumental on both sides.

The rule of the Four Hundred did not last long. Undermined by their own navy, divided by the formation of internal factions of moderates and extremists, and suspected of making overtures to the Spartans, they survived until shortly after the crucial battle of Cyzicus in 410 BCE, where the Athenian navy commanded by Alcibiades completely destroyed its Spartan opponents. This victory led to a domino effect that allowed Athens to retake control of a number of cities in the Hellespont. The defeated Spartans went so far as to make a peace offer, which was—not for the first time—soundly rejected.

How had Alcibiades managed such rapid changes of fortune on behalf of the Athenians? By treachery, as usual. We have already seen his scheming with Tissaphernes. In turn, he promised Persian support to the Athenians—in the form of a number of Phoenician ships to aid them against the Peloponnesians. As Thucydides puts it, "Thus Alcibiades frightened the Athenians with Tissaphernes, and Tissaphernes with the Athenians."[14]

The fact is that Athens won a series of battles between 411 and 406 BCE, either directly or indirectly because of Alcibiades's involvement. But even Alcibiades, of course, was not infallible. For one thing, he had overplayed the degree of support he had from Tissaphernes. For another, Tissaphernes turned out not to trust Alcibiades at all. After yet another battle won by the Athenians in part due to Alcibiades's intervention—at Abydos, in November 411 BCE—Alcibiades visited Tissaphernes, bearing gifts. He was promptly imprisoned because, explained Tissaphernes, the Persian king had ordered him to make war against the Athenians. Xenophon, who by now had taken over the chronicling of the war from Thucydides, tells us that Alcibiades managed to escape a month later, shortly thereafter delivering Byzantium to Athens by having an inside party open the gates to the Athenian troops.

Finally, in 407 BCE, Alcibiades felt confident enough to make his triumphal return to Athens, hailed as a hero and savior of the motherland—never mind his repeated disloyalty and even treachery. Xenophon relates that "[Alcibiades] was proclaimed general-in-chief with absolute authority, the people thinking that he was the man to recover for the state its former power; then, as his first act, he led out all his troops and conducted by land the procession of the Eleusinian Mysteries."[15]

The irony is strong here. Athens not only recalled and glorified the man who had been directly responsible for innumerable disasters befalling the city but allowed him to lead the very kind of religious rite that he had been condemned for mocking only a few years earlier. Nevertheless, Alcibiades's new glow did not last long. The following year, the Athenians suffered a minor naval defeat at Notium, which resulted in Alcibiades not being reelected general. He did not take it well and exiled himself, this time permanently. He would never again command Athenian troops.

His flamboyant career was now nearing its end. He sought the protection of the Persian court, as the famous Athenian general Themistocles had done a generation earlier. In fact, he compared himself directly to Themistocles, boasting that he would be of even greater service to the Persian king, Artaxerxes. But the Spartans this time were determined to do away with Alcibiades once and for all. Plutarch tells us that it was Critias— Plato's cousin and one of the Thirty Tyrants who had by now been installed by the Spartans to govern a defeated Athens— who initiated the final chapter of Alcibiades's life.

Critias argued to the Spartan general Lysander that Athens would not remain docile toward Lacedaemon so long as Alcibiades was alive. Lysander was apparently unconvinced but received direct orders from Sparta to finally eliminate Alcibiades. The Spartans might have felt the same as Critias or simply wanted to appease their king, Agis, who was still fuming because Alcibiades had seduced his wife. Whatever the reason, it was Lysander who wrote to the Persian satrap Pharnabazus and asked for the deed to be done. Pharnabazus in turn engaged his brother, Magaeus, and his uncle, Sousamithras.[16]

They caught up with Alcibiades in Phrygia, in modern central Anatolia, where he was staying with his mistress, the courtesan Timandra, presumably on his way to offer his services to Artaxerxes. Plutarch says that Alcibiades had a disturbing dream, a vision of what was about to happen. The party sent to kill him surrounded his house yet did not dare approach, setting fire to it instead. Alcibiades realized what was happening, wrapped his cloak around his left arm, and rushed out, sword in hand, yelling out his battle cry. He was so fearsome that the "barbarians" scattered in panic. Once they had gained enough distance, however, they rained down arrows and javelins on him.

At least, that's one version of his death. Another, also given by Plutarch, is a bit more mundane. True to form, on his way to the Persian court, Alcibiades had seduced a local girl. Her brothers were not amused, and they were the ones who set fire to the house and killed him with arrows.[17] He died in 404 BCE, the same year that Athens unconditionally surrendered to Sparta.

What are we to make of Alcibiades's life and especially, concerning our quest in this book, his character? Let's turn to two authoritative ancient commentators who studied the case closely: Thucydides and Plutarch.

THUCYDIDES ON ALCIBIADES

Thucydides is our major source on the entire Peloponnesian conflict, followed by Xenophon, who picked up the narrative where his predecessor abruptly left off, though he shifted the perspective significantly and looked at events more from the Spartan point of view. While Xenophon, as we shall soon see, is crucial for our understanding of Socrates (together with Plato, of course), Thucydides is equally crucial for our understanding of Alcibiades. Not only were the two contemporaries, but they met several times, and some of Thucydides's inside takes on a number of episodes during the war come directly from his conversations with Alcibiades.

Unlike Plutarch, Thucydides doesn't provide us with a clear and compact summary of his views on Alcibiades and indeed would probably have recoiled from the notion. He was a historian, not a moralist. Then again, he does pepper his narrative with critical commentaries about the war, the different parties involved, and even a number of the specific individuals who played major roles in the conflict. His comments on Alcibiades are sparse, but they nevertheless help us put together quite a convincing picture of Alcibiades's character.

For instance, the first mention of Alcibiades by Thucydides occurs in book V of *The History of the Peloponnesian War*, where we read that Alcibiades would have been thought young in any other city and that he was influential "by reason of his high descent."[18] In other words, he would not have had the impact he had, at least early on, if not for his family relations—both his biological family, the controversial Alcmaeonidae, and his adoptive one, that of Pericles, the unquestioned leader of Athens at the beginning of the war. Apparently that is yet another thing that has not changed much over the millennia: One way to forge your path in the world is to be lucky enough to know the right people; better yet if you are part of their family. This section in the *History* is immediately followed by a detailed account of the episode in which Alcibiades tricks the Spartan delegation to Athens into contradicting themselves, thereby losing credibility, embarrassing Nicias, and paving the way for Alcibiades's own scheme. While Thucydides abstains from any direct judgment, the overall picture he paints is definitely not flattering to Alcibiades, who comes across as a warmonger and a trickster.

When we come to the beginning of the fateful Sicilian expedition, Thucydides abandons any scruples he might have had and outright tells us what he thinks of Alcibiades:

> The most enthusiastic supporter of the expedition was Alcibiades the son of Cleinias; he was determined to oppose Nicias, who was always his political enemy and had just now spoken of him in disparaging terms; but the desire to command was even a stronger motive with him. He was hoping that he might be the conqueror of Sicily and Carthage; and that success would repair his private fortunes, and gain him money as well as glory. He had a great position among the citizens and was devoted to horse-racing and other pleasures which outran his means. And in the end his wild courses went far to ruin the Athenian state.[19]

The portrait that comes across in these few lines is damning indeed: Alcibiades is dissolute, he pushes Athens to war in part to escape from financial distress, he wants the command for self-aggrandizing reasons, and he will be a major cause of the fall of his city. The fact that this bit is immediately followed by the rendition of Alcibiades's speech does not help at all since, as we've seen, he is quoted as emphasizing his exploits at the Olympic Games and the lavish way in which he celebrated them—not exactly the sort of thing one wishes to hear from a serious statesman who is attempting to convince his fellow citizens to embark on a costly and perilous war against a strong opponent. Moreover, we get a direct taste of Alcibiades's arrogance when he says, "And where is the injustice, if I or any one who feels his own superiority to another refuses to be on a level with him?"[20]

After he defects to Sparta, Alcibiades gives a speech to his new friends, again reported by Thucydides and again not flattering at all. In fact, he is presented as a bit of a Sophist when he redefines democracy not as the government of the people but as any institution opposed to tyranny. That way he can pass himself, and his whole family, off as supporters of "democracy," while in fact they are no such thing. This is the same speech in which he boldly lies about the intentions of the Athenians in embarking on their expedition against Syracuse, intentions that he inflates significantly in order to make the threat seem even greater to his Lacedaemonian hosts. The irony is that what he describes to them are *his own* ambitions, not those of the city of Athens. Alcibiades concludes that speech with his treacherous suggestion that the Spartans occupy Decelea, which, as we have seen, was one of the single most destructive moves against Athens in the entire war.

Thucydides later slips in another negative comment on Alcibiades's character when he writes about Alcibiades successfully convincing several Ionian cities to rebel against Athens. Alcibiades makes a point of beating the Spartans to Miletus in order to secure for himself the "glory" of what amounts to a broad conspiracy against his own city. However, his success is short-lived because he gets into trouble at Sparta and has to secure asylum with the Persian Tissaphernes. Here too Thucydides reports the facts but also goes on to comment that the advice Alcibiades is now giving to the Persians is not, in fact, in order to help them but has the ulterior motive of persuading the Athenians to recall him from exile. No matter what the circumstances or whom he was allegedly working for, Alcibiades always first and foremost looks out for number one.

Some people do see clearly through Alcibiades's schemes. The Athenian general Phrynichus, Thucydides recounts, calls Alcibiades out in public, in front of the troops assembled at Samos, and openly states that Alcibiades does not care about what government is in power in Athens—oligarchy or democracy—so long as the government is friendly to him. It would be nice to think that Phrynichus himself is above such base behavior, but the historical fact is that he in turn betrayed the Athenians shortly thereafter, when it became convenient for him. In the end, he could not get away with it because he was outmaneuvered by none other than Alcibiades.

The last mention of Alcibiades in *The History of the Peloponnesian War* concerns yet another deception when our hero tries to convince the Athenians that he is great pals with Tissaphernes, who—he tells them—will certainly bring into the conflict, on the side of Athens, a number of Phoenician ships. Tissaphernes, in fact, has no intention of doing anything of the kind, and Alcibiades likely knows it. But he needs to overplay his hand in order to sell himself to his compatriots. Once again.

PLUTARCH ON ALCIBIADES

Unlike Thucydides, Plutarch embraces the role of moralist. His histories are explicitly meant to convey a better understanding of the moral character of a number of people who have had a significant impact on humanity's paths. Indeed, it is the desire for a deeper grasp of the vagaries of human character that motivates Plutarch to write his famous *Parallel Lives*. In each section of this seminal classical text, Plutarch compares a figure from ancient Greece with one from ancient Rome, for example, the Greek Pericles with the Roman Fabius Maximus. As Plutarch explains at the beginning of his life of Alexander the Great,

> I do not tell of all the famous actions of these men, nor even speak exhaustively at all in each particular case.... For it is not Histories that I am writing, but Lives; and in the most illustrious deeds there is not always a manifestation of virtue or vice, nay, a slight thing like a phrase or a jest often makes a greater revelation of character than battles when thousands fall.... Accordingly, just as painters get the likenesses in their portraits from the face and the expression of the eyes, wherein the character shows itself, but make very little account of the other parts of the body, so I must be permitted to devote myself rather to the signs of the soul in men, and by means of these to portray the life of each, leaving to others the description of their great contests.[21]

Given this preface, it is interesting to note that in the *Lives*, Plutarch compares Alcibiades with the possibly mythical figure of Gaius Marcius Coriolanus. It is not difficult to see why. Coriolanus, if he actually existed, was a contemporary of Themistocles, the Athenian general who defeated the Persians and was then exiled by his people and served under the Persian king Artaxerxes I. According to legend, Coriolanus was a young officer serving in the Roman army under the consul Postumus Cominius Auruncus. In 493 BCE, he participated in the Roman siege of the Volscian town of Corioli (hence his nickname). The unexpected reinforcement of the Volscians by a contingent from nearby Antium put the Romans in dire straits. Coriolanus took the initiative, fighting bravely, if recklessly, with a small contingent of trusted comrades, and managed to repel the Volscian reinforcements and dramatically charge on his horse through the town's gate. The stupefied inhabitants of Coriolis then capitulated, and the town fell into Roman hands.

Coriolanus became an instant hero in Rome, surpassing even the fame of his commander. But only two years later, things took a bad turn for him. He was an insufferable aristocrat, constantly attempting to undermine the interests of the plebeians. Rome was then recovering from a grain shortage; new provisions were imported from Sicily, and the Senate had to decide how to allocate them. Coriolanus proposed that distribution to the plebeians should be contingent on repealing a number of reforms that had just been passed three years earlier in response to the so-called first *secessio plebis* of 494 BCE, essentially a strike aiming to obtain better living conditions for poor people.

Even Coriolanus's own colleagues in the Senate thought that his proposal was too harsh, and the people were understandably upset. He went from hero to villain practically overnight. The tribunes of the plebeians, who had significant power during the Republic, put Coriolanus on trial. The other senators were ready to argue for acquittal, or at least for a lenient sentence, but Coriolanus disdained the proceedings and refused to appear at the trial. As a result, he was predictably condemned in absentia.

In order to escape the death sentence, Coriolanus went into exile, seeking asylum with none other than the Volsci, the very people he'd valiantly defeated only a few years earlier. The Volscian leader Attius Tullus Aufidius welcomed him into his home, and the two of them concocted a plan to convince the

Volscian leaders to end their truce with Rome, raise a new army, and invade again. Together, Coriolanus and Aufidius proved invincible even for the Romans. They quickly conquered a number of Roman towns, including Corioli, expelling the colonists.

They then marched on Rome itself, camping just five miles outside the city and preparing to lay siege to it. The Volscian forces set out to devastate the Roman countryside, with Coriolanus directing his new allies to stay away from patrician properties and focus instead on the plebeians in order to avenge himself for the indignity of having been put on trial by their tribune.

Rome was at the mercy of Coriolanus and Aufidius, and the Senate sent ambassadors to negotiate a truce. They were twice rejected. Roman priests were then asked to intercede, but they too were turned away. At this point, Plutarch says (and Shakespeare dramatizes), Coriolanus's own mother, Veturia (called Volumnia by Shakespeare, who possibly confused her with Coriolanus's wife), went to the Volscian camp at the head of a group of women—an unprecedented event in Roman history. Coriolanus was finally moved by the pleas of his mother and his wife and lifted the siege, a decision that did not make the Volscians happy in the least. This time, it was Aufidius who persuaded his fellow citizens to put Coriolanus on trial and to arrange for his assassination before the proceedings were over.

We can see why Plutarch pairs Alcibiades with Coriolanus in his *Lives*, as the parallels between them are obvious. Both men were dashing and brilliant, and they managed to make a mark on their respective cities early in their lives. Both were reckless, and both had a disdain for the common people. Most importantly, of course, neither deigned (or dared) to stand their own trial, preferring not just exile but switching to the enemy.

Both caused great injury to their countries, and finally, both were assassinated by their new allies, whom they had managed to betray in turn.

At the end of his *Lives* of Alcibiades and Coriolanus, Plutarch directly compares the two, especially in terms of their characters and virtues—or lack thereof. When considering them as statesmen, rather than soldiers, Plutarch appears to have a preference for Alcibiades, even though he roundly criticizes both men. True, Alcibiades was dissolute and vulgar and flattered the multitudes in order to pursue his own objectives. But Coriolanus was ungracious and prideful, which leads Plutarch to comment, "Neither course, then, is to be approved; although the man who seeks to win the people by his favors is less blameworthy than those who heap insults on the multitude, in order to avoid the appearance of trying to win them. For it is a disgrace to flatter the people for the sake of power; but to get power by acts of terror, violence, and oppression, is not only a disgrace, it is also an injustice."[22]

In terms of their modus operandi, Plutarch notes that both Alcibiades and Coriolanus achieved their objectives by deceit, the former by tricking the Spartan ambassadors to Athens and the latter by inducing the Roman Senate to expel the Volsci from the Ludi Romani, the Roman equivalent of the Olympic Games, and in so doing stirring up ill will between the parties. However, Plutarch adds, the results of these actions were quite different. While Alcibiades managed to build a strong pro-Athenian alliance with Argos and Mantinea, the outcome of Coriolanus's actions decidedly damaged Rome. The reason for this difference was that Alcibiades was moved primarily by ambition and the struggle for political rivalry, whereas Coriolanus gave way to his anger. Anger, Plutarch notes, is a passion from which "no one ever gets a grateful return."[23]

Alcibiades and Coriolanus also behaved differently with respect to their countrymen when the opportunity for reconciliation came. The Greek showed goodwill to the Athenians as soon as they repented for the way they had treated him; indeed, he went on to secure a great number of victories on their behalf and even attempted to save Athens's fleet at the battle of Aegospotami, just before the final Athenian confrontation with Lysander. By contrast, Coriolanus showed no inclination to forgive the Romans when they sued for peace, relenting only when he saw his mother and his wife humiliate themselves in front of him. When they switched sides, again, the two men acted from different motives—none of them virtuous. Alcibiades, Plutarch reminds us, returned to the Athenians in part because he had a reasonable fear of the Spartans, who were in fact plotting against his life (though they were doing so because he had been incautious enough to sleep with their queen and impregnate her). By contrast, when Coriolanus betrayed the Volsci, he did so even though they had treated him with all honors and given him full command of their army.

Then again, the comparison doesn't always favor Alcibiades. Take, for instance, how Plutarch describes the two men's relationship with money. Alcibiades craved money and could be bribed because of his desire to obtain more of it, only to dissipate it all on luxuries. Coriolanus couldn't care less about wealth, which made him incorruptible. However, even this positive trait did not endear him to the multitudes since they understood very well that his attitude toward them was the result of scorn and insolence rather than the pursuit of personal gain.

In terms of their ability to persuade others, the two couldn't have been more different. Alcibiades knew how to ingratiate himself with people and bring them around to his point of view.

Coriolanus had no clue how to do anything of the sort, which made even his virtues come across as obnoxious. This difference, says Plutarch, may explain why Alcibiades was consistently successful when at home and suffered only when he was away from Athens and could not confront his accusers directly. Coriolanus was condemned by the Romans while he was in Rome and killed by the Volscians while he was in their presence. Obviously he was not much of a persuader.

Near the end of his comparative analysis of Alcibiades and Coriolanus, Plutarch makes additional insightful psychological observations. He notes that Alcibiades very openly admitted that he wanted to be liked and behaved accordingly, courting the favors of the multitude in any way possible. Coriolanus professed not to care about honors and accordingly paid no attention to the crowd. Yet he felt seriously injured when recognition was withdrawn from him by that very crowd. Plutarch comments, "Surely he who least courts the people's favor, ought least to resent their neglect, since vexation over failure to receive their honors is most apt to spring from an excessive longing after them."[24]

Notwithstanding an almost invariably unfavorable comparison with Alcibiades, Plutarch concludes that Coriolanus was the more admirable of the two because he displayed the virtues of temperance and disregard for wealth, unlike Alcibiades, who most definitely sought wealth at every turn and was the furthest one can imagine from a temperate man.

The verdict seems clear: Socrates failed in his attempt to instill virtue in Alcibiades, a failure that Socrates himself clearly foresaw early on, when Alcibiades was still young and the two were discoursing about what makes a good statesman. In part to better understand this failure and in part to better grasp what

Socrates was trying to do in Athens, we need to examine both his life and his philosophy more closely. This will in turn put us in a better position to follow successive attempts by other philosophers—from Plato to Aristotle to Seneca—to teach the statesmen of their day. Therefore, let us now turn our attention to the famous, or infamous, gadfly of Athens.

4

THE GADFLY OF ATHENS

For if you kill me you will not easily find another like me, who, if I may use such a ludicrous figure of speech, am a sort of gadfly, given to the state by the God.

—PLATO, *APOLOGY*

THE SOCRATIC PROBLEM

A few years ago in Brooklyn, I went to see *Socrates*, a play by Tim Blake Nelson, with the title character played by the awesome Michael Stuhlbarg. The performance was almost three hours long, yet it felt as if I wasn't aware of the time because I couldn't take my eyes off Stuhlbarg whenever he was onstage. Nor could I possibly avoid being transported to the time and place of Socrates, in part because of the stunning set designed by Scott Pask, which featured walls decorated with passages from Pericles's funeral oration—with the lettering in ancient Greek.

Nelson's play began with a young Aristotle (played by Niall Cunningham) being introduced to Plato (Teagle F. Bougere) and inquiring rather pointedly about why the Athenians killed their most famous philosopher. Plato's explanation led the

audience to a scene taken from the *Symposium*, the by now familiar Platonic dialogue in which the playwright Aristophanes explains the concept of soulmates. Socrates says he was instructed
in love by the philosopher Diotima, and a flamboyant Alcibiades crashes the party, telling the audience that—despite his best
attempts—he was unable to (sexually) seduce his mentor.

From there, Nelson's play moved on to the charges against
Socrates and the beginning of his trial for impiety, or worship-
ing foreign gods, and the corruption of Athenian youth. Socrates's accusers—eerie stand-ins for modern rabble-rousing
populists—spoke first. Then the man himself passionately defended his self-appointed role as gadfly to the rich and powerful.

At this point, the play alternated between the trial and a
number of scenes from selected Platonic dialogues that portrayed Socrates in action with his friends and opponents. In
the end, of course, Socrates was convicted. When offered the
opportunity to suggest an alternative punishment to the death
penalty, instead of proposing exile—as expected—he said that
the Athenians should offer him free housing and a stipend in
thanks for all the work he had done for them and would continue to do until his last breath. No wonder, as Plato pointed
out onstage, he was condemned to death by more votes than
found him guilty in the first round.

The famous death scene ended the play and was poignant
not least because we saw the distress of Socrates's friends as well
as of his wife, Xanthippe (played by Miriam A. Hyman). We
also watched Socrates's last moments, which showed how hor-
ribly painful death by hemlock actually is. The philosopher's last
words were delivered to one of his close friends: "Crito, I owe
the sacrifice of a rooster to Asclepius; will you pay that debt and
not neglect to do so?" Plato explains this reference to young

Aristotle: Asclepius is the god of healing, and that was all Socrates ever wanted to do in his life.

I went to see *Socrates* for a number of reasons. One was that I was curious about the fact that the production was the centerpiece of the 2019 Onassis Festival on democracy. Socrates himself wasn't exactly a fan of the ancient Athenian implementation of the concept, but he also did not support the inter-reign of the tyrants who were put in charge by Sparta after the end of the Peloponnesian War. Rather, true to character, he went around questioning the politicians of the day and was put to death as thanks for his troubles. There was a poignant moment in the play when one of his accusers foamed at the mouth while shouting that Socrates was a traitor for daring to question democracy. The philosopher responded that no idea is sacred and that everything needs to be questioned, especially if it appears that people hide behind an idea without understanding it or are blind to its limitations.

In modern times, we are once again witnessing the trouble with democracy that Plato highlighted in his writings: It has a tendency to slide into tyranny. Whether we might conceive of a better system remains to be seen. But questioning the institution and its specific implementations is a must for any thinking person who is truly interested in justice and human flourishing. And Socrates was nothing if not bent on questioning things.

As we know, Socrates's regular antagonists were the Sophists, who—at least in Plato's caricature—would have found themselves at home in our modern world of alternative facts and fake news. After all, they argued that one can convincingly defend any point of view as well as its opposite, implying that there is no truth in human affairs. Man is the measure of all things, and so forth. By contrast, Socrates—whom the Oracle at Delphi had declared to be the wisest man in all Greece—did not claim to have the truth but was stubbornly searching for it, in open defiance of the Sophists' attitude.

The sage of Athens himself did not think he was wise and set out to demonstrate that the Oracle was wrong. In order to do so, he started to question the most important (and self-important) men of his city, discovering, to his astonishment, that they only pretended to know things and perhaps were even convinced by their own pretensions. As modern political philosopher Harry Frankfurt would put it, they were bullshitters.[1] A major lesson to be drawn from both the play and the historical accounts of Socrates by Plato and Xenophon is that people—be they fourth-century BCE Athenians or denizens of any country in the twenty-first century—readily fall for bullshit. Moreover, when bullshitters are called to task, their tendency is to swat the gadflies that annoy them.

That said, at the end of Nelson's play, I was confronted with the so-called Socratic problem: the question of how much of what we think we know about the philosopher corresponds to the actual historical figure. The short answer is that we will never know, but a more nuanced one is that we can triangulate among the various available sources, doing our best to resolve their inconsistencies so that something as close as possible to the real Socrates may emerge from the fog of time.

Our major sources for Socrates's life and character are Plato and Xenophon, both of whom were his students. We also have a number of references to Socrates by Aristotle (who was Plato's student) as well as Antisthenes and Aeschines of Sphettos, among others. We know something about Socrates's youth because of the travel journals of Ion of Chios. And we have a number of satirical treatments of Socrates, the most famous being Aristophanes's *The Clouds*.

A notorious cause of the Socratic problem is that Plato—by far our chief source—clearly uses his mentor as a character in his philosophical dialogues; Paul Johnson in his book *Socrates: A Man for Our Times* refers to this hybrid creature as "Platsoc." Even so, scholars think that some Socratic dialogues by Plato were written earlier and are more likely to reflect Socrates's actual thinking, for instance, *Apology*, recounting Socrates's speech in his defense at his trial; *Charmides*, where Socrates discusses temperance and self-knowledge; *Euthydemus*, with Socrates engaging in debate with two Sophists; and perhaps the most Socratic of all Socratic dialogues, *Euthyphro*, which inquires about the nature of piety. Ironically, some of the least Socratic, so-called middle and late dialogues by Plato happen to be among the best known and most influential: *Symposium*, featuring Alcibiades as well as Socrates discussing *érōs*; *Phaedo*, recounting Socrates's last hours in prison; and *Republic*, in which Socrates is presented as very critical of democracy.

Although difficult, it is possible to at least partially and tentatively separate Socrates's own philosophy from Plato's. But—most importantly for our project here—what do we know about Socrates's character? Who was he as a human being? What was he really like? Plato, interested primarily in philosophy, offers only indirect hints, such as when Alcibiades describes Socrates's valor at the battles of Delium and Potidaea. It is Xenophon, a historian who does not really have any particular philosophical axe to grind, who gifts us with the most vivid, and seemingly realistic, portrait of Socrates in action. Let us take a closer look using Xenophon's *Memorabilia*, a book so striking that Zeno of Citium—the founder of Stoicism—decided to become a philosopher as soon as he heard a bookseller declaiming a few pages from it.

SOCRATES IMPARTS A LESSON TO HIS SON

Throughout *Memorabilia*, Xenophon presents us with a number of short vignettes from Socrates's life, situations where he is always interacting with some fellow Athenian and perennially asking probing questions. Xenophon's writing style is, in my opinion, far more enjoyable than Plato's, and we have a definite sense that we are encountering the real Socrates, not just Plat-soc. Indeed, in some cases, Xenophon's portrayal of Socrates's approach seems to be at odds with the portrayal that emerges from the Platonic dialogues. Frankly, Xenophon's version often makes more sense to me.

A first telling episode is found in book II, which relates a conversation between Socrates and his eldest son, Lamprocles, regarding the latter's attitude toward his mother, Xanthippe. Lamprocles has been complaining about Xanthippe, who is too strict with him and, in his opinion, doesn't really care about him. Socrates begins by addressing Lamprocles as follows: "Tell me, my boy, do you know that some men are called ungrateful?"[2]

It's a classic Socratic trick question, and Lamprocles falls for it. He responds, yes, he does. Socrates then asks if he knows why such people are so labeled, and the son dutifully provides a definition of ingratitude. Socrates goes on to suggest that being ungrateful is a type of injustice, and again his son agrees. At this point the father adds, "'Therefore the greater the benefits received the greater the injustice of not showing gratitude?' He agreed again. 'Now what deeper obligation can we find than that of children to their parents?'"[3]

And you can begin to see the outline of the trap that the philosopher is setting even for his own son: We are shifting from a general discussion of ingratitude, including an agreement that it is a form of injustice, to the specific case of the relationship between children and their parents. Socrates then comments on why people marry and have children, explaining to Lamprocles how gender roles are understood in ancient Athens. When he comes to the role of women, he says, "The woman conceives and bears her burden in travail, risking her life, and giving of her own food; and, with much labour, having endured to the end and brought forth her child, she rears and cares for it."[4] A mother then proceeds to selflessly give to her offspring, providing them with whatever she thinks they want and need. And of course this is not limited to food but encompasses anything the mother is able to teach. If she is in no position to teach, then she looks for someone who can, all in the interest of her sons and daughters.

Lamprocles reluctantly agrees but complains that even so, nobody can put up with Xanthippe's vile temper. He adds that it is harder to bear his mother than even a wild beast. Socrates, feigning surprise, asks whether Xanthippe has ever bitten or kicked him, as a wild beast would. "'Oh no, but she says things one wouldn't listen to for anything in the world.' 'Well, how much trouble do you think you have given her by your peevish words and froward acts day and night since you were a little child; and how much pain when you were ill?'"[5]

After having disposed of the wild-beast analogy, Socrates asks his son whether it is more difficult for him to listen to his mother than for an actor to be abused onstage by another actor, who obviously doesn't mean it and is playing an assigned role. He continues, "'Unless, indeed, you suppose that your mother is maliciously set against you?' 'Oh no, I don't think that.' Then Socrates exclaimed: 'So this mother of yours is kindly disposed towards you; she nurses you devotedly in sickness and sees that you want for nothing; more than that, she prays the gods to bless you abundantly and pays vows on your behalf; and yet you say she is a trial! It seems to me that, if you can't endure a mother like her, you can't endure a good thing.'"[6]

By now Lamprocles has been forced by way of Socratic logic to agree that ingratitude is a form of injustice, that his mother has his best interests in mind, that her words can certainly be borne with equanimity, and that he, Lamprocles, apparently is afflicted by the peculiar problem of not being able to endure a good thing!

But Socrates is not quite done. He asks his son whether he wishes to please at least some people, perhaps such as his neighbor, in order to develop a relationship of mutual aid. Lamprocles says he does. He then also admits that he would cultivate the goodwill of a traveling companion in order to make friends, not enemies. Ah, says Socrates, and yet you deny that mere courtesy is due to your mother, who is the one who loves you most of all? He concludes, "Therefore, my boy, if you are prudent, you will pray the gods to pardon your neglect of your mother, lest they in turn refuse to be kind to you, thinking you an ingrate; and you will beware of men, lest all cast you out, perceiving that you care nothing for your parents, and in the end you are found to be without a friend. For, should men suppose you to be ungrateful to your parents, none would think you would be grateful for any kindness he might show you."[7]

Here, we see again the famous Socratic method, or *elenchus*, at work. The method is still used today in classrooms, especially in philosophy and law. As we've seen when discussing the dialogues between Socrates and Alcibiades, we can think of the *elenchus* as a negative way to arrive at a conclusion by progressively discarding notions that don't seem to work. Typically,

Socrates and his interlocutor set a topic—in this case, Xanthippe's allegedly insufferable behavior toward Lamprocles. Then Socrates begins to pose questions aimed at uncovering the other person's underlying assumptions, for instance Lamprocles's obvious underestimation of the positive and burdensome role his mother has already played in his life. At some point, the questioning highlights some inconsistency or contradiction in the interlocutor's position, as when Lamprocles is forced to reject the notion that his mother has been acting maliciously toward him. After this, the line of questioning either ceases or resumes by considering a revised initial position, which is then subjected to the same procedure. This continues until Socrates reaches either a positive conclusion (as he does with Lamprocles) or, more often, a state of *aporia*, an impasse where no definite conclusion has been reached.

There probably are good reasons why Socratic dialogues frequently end in *aporia*. To begin with, Socrates always maintains that he is not a teacher but rather something closer to a midwife. He cannot instruct others because he is himself unwise (despite the clear statement to the contrary by the Oracle at Delphi). At best, he can help others arrive at certain conclusions. This is a valuable lesson for teachers of any time or place: Teaching is not a process by which instructors fill empty minds with their own notions. True teaching rather consists of gently guiding students, steering them away from fallacies and, slowly but surely, toward a better grasp of things and ideas. Students then own their conclusions, arrive at a better understanding, and are able to internalize notions rather than simply regurgitate someone else's opinion.

Socrates appears to have been rather skeptical of the possibility of ultimate human knowledge, as opposed to well-reasoned yet tentative opinion—though this is particularly clear in Plato's *Phaedo*, which is not one of the early dialogues and in which it is therefore more difficult to distinguish Socrates from Platsoc. Regardless, the *elenchus* seems to be designed to chip away at untruths, so to speak, in the hope of drawing ever closer to the underlying truth. I am reminded of the Italian Renaissance sculptor Michelangelo, who said that he wasn't really creating his statues but was just removing the marble that enclosed them, thus bringing them to light. Perhaps something like this analogy occurred to Socrates. He was, after all, a trained stonemason.

SOCRATES AND HOW TO GIVE ADVICE TO POLITICIANS

It is often said that Socrates did not put forth his own opinions during his conversations with friends, acquaintances, and assorted Sophists. This is somewhat, though not entirely, true of the Platonic dialogues, but it isn't the Socrates we encounter in Xenophon. That Socrates has clear opinions and does not hold back from dispensing advice. Two contrasting examples are found in book III of *Memorabilia*, and they are highly pertinent to our concerns because they deal with whether someone should embark on a political career. Here Socrates gives opposite advice to his two interlocutors, strongly discouraging the enthusiastic Glaucon while at the same time just as strongly nudging forward the reluctant Charmides.

Glaucon was Plato's older brother. He appears in a major role in the *Republic*, where he asks Socrates why we shouldn't do whatever pleases us if we can get away with it. At the time of the dialogue reported by Xenophon, Glaucon is only twenty years old and is bent on a career as an orator and politician. Indeed, he wants to become head of the Athenian state—just as Alcibiades does. Socrates comments that this is indeed a fine aspiration, which will make Glaucon's father proud and will make Glaucon himself well known throughout Greece and possibly beyond. However, "Socrates asked, 'Well, Glaucon, as you want to win honor, is it not obvious that you must benefit your city?' 'Most certainly.' 'Pray don't be reticent, then; but tell us how you propose to begin your services to the state.'...Glaucon remained dumb, apparently considering for the first time how to begin."[8]

This is obviously not a good start, though one cannot but feel that a number of modern politicians continue to imitate Glaucon's thoughtless approach. Socrates then probes Glaucon on a series of policy issues, asking him, for instance, whether he is acquainted with the sources and amounts of the city's revenues. Glaucon admits ignorance but suggests that the subject isn't that important since one can make the city's enemies pay for its expenses, again reminding us of recent political figures pretty much the world over. But Socrates isn't persuaded: "'In order to advise her whom to fight, it is necessary to know the strength of the city and of the enemy, so that, if the city be stronger, one may recommend her to go to war, but if weaker than the enemy, may persuade her to beware.' 'You are right.' 'First, then, tell us the naval and military strength of our city, and then that of her enemies.' 'No, of course I can't tell you out of my head.'"[9]

Socrates then inquires about Glaucon's plans for the various Athenian garrisons scattered throughout the territory controlled by the city, suggesting that he may want to optimize their distribution, as some are well placed, whereas others are not. Here Glaucon gets into further trouble, stating that he intends to eliminate all garrisons, as they are a waste of money. Socrates replies, "'But if you do away with the garrisons, don't you think that anyone will be at liberty to rob us openly? However, have you been on a tour of inspection, or how do you know that they are badly maintained?' 'By guess-work.' 'Then shall we wait to offer advice on this question too until we really know, instead of merely guessing?' 'Perhaps it would be better.'"[10]

Socrates continues his push by bringing up the issue of the silver mines, a major source of wealth for Athens at the time. Of course Glaucon has not bothered to visit them, so he knows nothing about the subject. Next Socrates asks whether Glaucon has a good estimate of how long the grain reserves will last, as those are crucial to feed the city. The response is that that task is too overwhelming, and Glaucon didn't feel like carrying it out.

Socrates at this point chides his interlocutor, reminding him that if one wishes to take charge of a household, one must bother with exactly the sort of details that Glaucon has so far neglected when it comes to affairs of state. Perhaps, Socrates suggests with not entirely veiled irony, Glaucon could begin by taking care of his uncle's house, which clearly needs work. Only after cutting his teeth on that small task should he contemplate the possibility of being in charge of all the households in the city. "'Well, I could do something for uncle's household if only he would listen to me.' 'What? You can't persuade your uncle, and yet you suppose you will be able to persuade all the Athenians, including your uncle, to listen to you? Pray take care, Glaucon, that your daring ambition doesn't lead to a fall! Don't you see how risky it is to say or do what you don't understand?'"[11]

That apparently does the trick, and Glaucon postpones his dream of becoming head of state. In fact, he never became one. Instead, he fought valiantly at the battle of Megara, at the height of the Peloponnesian War in 424 BCE, the year after the above conversation took place. He later became a competent musician, as Socrates attests in the *Republic*.

If only modern politicians had someone like Socrates to point out how ridiculously unprepared they are for their chosen career, and—more crucially—if they were as ready as Glaucon to accept such counsel, the world would be a far better place. However, let us contrast the above episode with the next one, concerning Charmides, who happened to be Glaucon's son, which means that this second dialogue took place significantly later. Here Socrates does the opposite of what he did with Glaucon, positively encouraging a recalcitrant but obviously virtuous individual to enter public life: "Seeing that Glaucon's son, Charmides, was a respectable man and far more capable than the politicians of the day, and nevertheless shrank from speaking in the assembly and taking a part in politics, [Socrates] said: 'Tell me, Charmides, what would you think of a man who was capable of gaining a victory in the great games and consequently of winning honor for himself and adding to his country's fame in the Greek world, and yet refused to compete?' 'I should think him a poltroon and a coward, of course.'"[12]

When Charmides realizes that Socrates is talking about him, he asks what makes Socrates think that he, Charmides, would be good at public speaking. Socrates replies that he has seen how powerful men listen to Charmides's advice when given in private. "'A private conversation is a very different thing from a crowded debate, Socrates.' 'But, you know, a man who is good at figures counts as well in a crowd as in solitude; and those who play the harp best in private excel no less in a crowd.'"[13]

Good point. Socrates ends the encounter with a heartfelt exhortation to Charmides to join the ranks of the city's decision makers: "Don't refuse to face this duty then: strive more earnestly to pay heed to yourself; and don't neglect public affairs, if you have the power to improve them. If they go well, not only the people, but your friends and you yourself at least as much as they will profit."[14]

Charmides did go into politics, though he had the bad luck of serving under the infamous Thirty Tyrants, as did Socrates himself, after the end of the Peloponnesian War. He died in battle at Munichia in 403 BCE.

The point that particularly interests us about these two episodes is the relationship between philosophy and politics that emerges from the exchanges. Plato argues in the *Republic* that a just state can be achieved only once philosophers are in charge—though by "philosophers" he certainly didn't mean academicians such as me but rather people who practiced philosophy as "the art of living." Short of that, philosophers should mentor and advise politicians.

These are two models that we will explore in the next two chapters. To his credit, Plato attempted to practice what he preached and almost lost his life by order of the tyrant of Syracuse, Dionysius II, as we shall soon see. Aristotle—whom we will also encounter shortly—fared a bit better with Alexander in that he was not banished. But the historical record is open to interpretation regarding whether Alexander attempted to implement the philosophy of his mentor. Marcus Aurelius, yet another crucial historical figure whom we will examine closely, certainly did learn from his Stoic teachers, particularly Quintus Junius Rusticus, and tried his best to practice those philosophical teachings throughout his reign as emperor.

After reading Socrates's exchanges with Glaucon and Charmides, we may be puzzled by the philosopher's apparently unwavering support of Alcibiades, who surely resembled Glaucon far more than Charmides. But remember the dialogues that we discussed earlier and how Socrates rather vehemently accuses Alcibiades of willful and dangerous stupidity for wanting to enter politics to seek personal glory rather than the common good. Socrates remained a steadfast friend of Alcibiades; however, his friendship did not come with an endorsement of the younger man's approach to the res publica—what the Romans called the public thing.

SOCRATES, SOPHISTRY, AND STATESMANSHIP

This book is, in part, about statesmanship, so it is appropriate to see what sort of advice Socrates explicitly gives on this topic in book IV of Xenophon's *Memorabilia*. The passage features a young fellow named Euthydemus. You will appreciate, I think, why the conversation reported by Xenophon should be mandatory reading for any politician of the modern era. They (and we) could benefit from it immensely. The episode begins with Xenophon giving us a portrait of Euthydemus as rather full of himself: "[Socrates] was informed that Euthydemus, the handsome, had formed a large collection of the works of celebrated poets and professors, and therefore supposed himself to be a prodigy of wisdom for his age, and was confident of surpassing all competitors in power of speech and action."[15]

Having heard of this, Socrates goes to see Euthydemus to jump-start the latter's critical thinking, as we would say today. He approaches the fellow and says, "If in the minor arts great achievement is impossible without competent masters, surely it is absurd to imagine that the art of statesmanship, the greatest of all accomplishments, comes to a man of its own accord."[16]

Apparently this first encounter failed to move Euthydemus from his arrogant assumption that he was worthy of leading the state just because he had amassed a collection of writings by others. A bit later the two meet again, and this time Socrates openly mocks Euthydemus by imagining what speech he will give at the Athenian Assembly in order to convince the members to take his advice seriously. The mock speech includes a series of analogies between statesmanship and other professions in which Socrates imagines how Euthydemus will make his case in front of an audience. For instance, if he wished to be appointed doctor, Socrates says, Euthydemus would go about it as follows: "Men of Athens, I have never yet studied medicine, nor sought to find a teacher among our physicians; for I have constantly avoided learning anything from the physicians, and even the appearance of having studied their art. Nevertheless I ask you to appoint me to the office of a physician, and I will endeavor to learn by experimenting on you."[17]

Obviously nobody would trust such a doctor. Then again, we often hear something very similar to this from modern politicians, especially those who actually brag of having no government experience. Yet people vote for them anyway, often with disastrous results.

As if this mockery were too subtle, Xenophon's Socrates states the situation more clearly:

"How strange it is," he said, "that those who want to play the harp or the flute, or to ride or to get skill in any similar accomplishment, work hard at the art they mean to master, and not by themselves but under the tuition of the most eminent professors, doing and bearing anything in their anxiety to do nothing without their teachers' guidance, just because that is the only way to become proficient: and yet, among those who want to shine as speakers in the Assembly and as statesmen, there are some who think that they will be able to do so on a sudden, by instinct, without training or study."[18]

Sound familiar? It should. Now, throughout all of this, Euthydemus avoids directly engaging with Socrates, remaining silent and apart from the company. But when he's had enough, he finally enters the dialogue:[19]

[Socrates] Surely, Euthydemus, you don't covet the kind of excellence that makes good statesmen and managers, competent rulers and benefactors of themselves and mankind in general?

[Euthydemus] Yes, I do, Socrates. That kind of excellence I greatly desire.

[Socrates] Why, it is the noblest kind of excellence, the greatest of arts that you covet, for it belongs to kings and is dubbed "kingly." However, have you reflected whether it be possible to excel in these matters without being a just man?

[Euthydemus] Yes, certainly; and it is, in fact, impossible to be a good citizen without justice.

[Socrates] Then tell me, have you got that?

[Euthydemus] Yes, Socrates, I think I can show myself to be as just as any man.

Euthydemus immediately falls for Socrates's standard bait: He agreed that in order to pursue his goal of statesmanship, he must possess a particular character trait, and now he is asked to provide a compelling definition of such trait in order to show that he knows what he is talking about. It will not go well.

That part of the dialogue—between IV.2.12 and IV.2.19—is worth reading in full as a classic example of the *elenchus*. As far as we are concerned here, it suffices to say that Socrates ends up compelling Euthydemus to admit that the very same thing can be termed just or unjust depending on the circumstances. For instance, deceiving a friend is normally unjust unless it is for his own benefit, say, to make sure that your friend does not commit suicide, to use a specific example brought up by Socrates. By the end of this bit, Euthydemus is properly confused about the subject matter and admits his confusion—which of course is the beginning of wisdom: "Nay, Socrates, I have lost all confidence in my answers; for all the opinions that I expressed before seem now to have taken an entirely different form."[20]

Socrates then suddenly appears to be changing the subject but in fact is simply shifting to a different angle while pursuing his intent to humble Euthydemus and show him that he has a lot more work to do than he thinks before he can embark on a political career:[21]

> [Socrates] Tell me, Euthydemus, have you ever been to Delphi?
>
> [Euthydemus] Yes, certainly; twice.
>
> [Socrates] Then did you notice somewhere on the temple the inscription "Know thyself"?
>
> [Euthydemus] I did.
>
> [Socrates] And did you pay no heed to the inscription, or did you attend to it and try to consider who you were?
>
> [Euthydemus] Indeed I did not; because I felt sure that I knew that already; for I could hardly know anything else if I did not even know myself.

But of course it turns out that Euthydemus does not really know himself at all, not in the manner that counts if the goal is to improve his character and wisely assess which career he should pursue. Many of us make the same mistake today: Just because we are acquainted with ourselves, because we have access to our inner thoughts and have lived with ourselves all our lives, we think we have a pretty good working knowledge of who we are. But such working knowledge is rather superficial. If we truly wish to know ourselves, we need to engage in critical self-reflection, ideally aided by friends or others who want to help and are not shy about pointing out our rationalizations and excuses. We all need our inner Socrates, as well as outer ones, if we can find them.

Why would the sort of self-knowledge advised by the Oracle at Delphi be a good thing? Socrates explains, "Is it not clear too that through self-knowledge men come to much good, and through self-deception to much harm?"[22] He continues, "Those who do not know and are deceived in their estimate of their own powers, are in the like condition with regard to other men and other human affairs. They know neither what they want, nor what they do, nor those with whom they have intercourse; but mistaken in all these respects, they miss the good and stumble into the bad."[23]

There is a whiff here of the Socratic notion that no one does evil on purpose but only through ignorance. Ignorance, in this context, is understood to mean lack of wisdom, the very same lack of wisdom that affects people such as Euthydemus or many modern politicians who don't see the point of following the Delphic injunction. Socrates then engages in another instance of the *elenchus* to show Euthydemus that he really doesn't have a clear idea of what is good and what is evil:[24]

[Socrates] Well, I may assume, I take it, that you know what things are good and what are evil?

[Euthydemus] Of course, for if I don't know so much as that, I must be worse than a slave.

[Socrates] Come then, state them for my benefit.

[Euthydemus] Well, that's a simple matter. First health in itself is, I suppose, a good, sickness an evil. Next the various causes of these two conditions—meat, drink, habits—are good or evil according as they promote health or sickness.

[Socrates] Then health and sickness too must be good when their effect is good, and evil when it is evil.

[Euthydemus] But when can health possibly be the cause of evil, or sickness of good?

[Socrates] Why, in many cases; for instance, a disastrous campaign or a fatal voyage: the able-bodied who go are lost, the weaklings who stay behind are saved.

[Euthydemus] True; but you see, in the successful adventures too the able-bodied take part, the weaklings are left behind.

[Socrates] Then since these bodily conditions sometimes lead to profit, and sometimes to loss, are they any more good than evil?

The fundamental point here is that what we so unreflectively think of as good (or evil), such as health, wealth, fame (or, conversely, sickness, poverty, anonymity), is actually morally neutral. What makes such things into something to be preferred (or dispreferred) is how one handles them. That is why the only true good for Socrates is wisdom, and the only true evil is lack of wisdom.

It is wisdom that allows us to make good use of externals, such as health, wealth, and fame. For Socrates, not even happiness—which is often presented even in modern times as an intrinsic good—qualifies because it depends on how we think of it:[25]

> [**Euthydemus**] Happiness seems to be unquestionably a good, Socrates.
>
> [**Socrates**] It would be so, Euthydemus, were it not made up of goods that are questionable.
>
> [**Euthydemus**] But what element in happiness can be called in question?
>
> [**Socrates**] None, provided we don't include in it beauty or strength or wealth or glory or anything of the sort.
>
> [**Euthydemus**] But of course we shall do that. For how can anyone be happy without them?
>
> [**Socrates**] Then of course we shall include the sources of much trouble to mankind. For many are ruined by admirers whose heads are turned at the sight of a pretty face; many are led by their strength to attempt tasks too heavy for them, and meet with serious evils; many by their wealth are corrupted, and fall victims to conspiracies; many through glory and political power have suffered great evils.

Again, the point is that what superficially, unreflectively appear to be "obvious" goods turn out to be anything but. Happiness—in Greek the word is *eudaimonia*—does not consist in possessing such goods but in using well whatever goods Fortune allows us. For once, though, the story has a happy ending, according to Xenophon:

Now many of those who were brought to this pass by Socrates, never went near him again and were regarded by him as mere blockheads. But Euthydemus guessed that he would never be of much account unless he spent as much time as possible with Socrates. Henceforward, unless obliged to absent himself, he never left him, and even began to adopt some of his practices. Socrates, for his part, seeing how it was with him, avoided worrying him, and began to expound very plainly and clearly the knowledge that he thought most needful and the practices that he held to be most excellent.[26]

The picture we get from this story is enlightening in several respects. It shows us a Socrates who doesn't behave like a gadfly for the sake of annoying people but rather to make them think more carefully and ultimately to help them become better human beings. It also shows that he sometimes succeeded in his efforts, as Euthydemus is a good counter to the failure that is Alcibiades.

IN DEFENSE OF SOCRATES

The *Memorabilia* begins with Xenophon wondering what possessed the Athenians to condemn Socrates on the well-known pair of charges: rejecting the gods acknowledged by the state while bringing in strange deities and corruption of youth.[27] His defense of Socrates against his compatriots provides us with valuable insights into the character of the philosopher and is therefore crucial to our discussion.

Xenophon begins by addressing the first charge and dismissing it on the basis of empirical observation: Socrates was known for making offers to the gods of Athens, both in the privacy of his home and publicly in temples.[28] Moreover, Socrates often said that he was following the counsel of the gods, which was given to him by way of appropriate signs. How could anyone be charged with impiety if he took advice from the gods and himself gave advice to others on the basis of those very same signs?[29] Xenophon then provides us with a rare and precious description of Socrates's typical day: "Socrates lived ever in the open; for early in the morning he went to the public prome-nades and training-grounds; in the forenoon he was seen in the market; and the rest of the day he passed just where most people were to be met: he was generally talking, and anyone might listen."[30]

Xenophon also states quite clearly[31] that Socrates did not in-dulge in metaphysical speculation, what he calls philosophizing on "the nature of the universe," yet another reason it is bizarre to accuse his friend of impiety. This is interesting in part because it confirms that Socrates turned away from the broad interests of Presocratics such as Thales and Heraclitus and focused instead on ethics and what we would today call political philosophy. Which, of course, is what really got him into trouble with cer-tain exponents of the Athenian aristocracy: "His own conver-sation was ever of human beings. The problems he discussed were, what is godly, what is ungodly; what is beautiful, what is ugly; what is just, what is unjust; what is prudence, what is mad-ness; what is courage, what is cowardice; what is a state, what is a statesman; what is government and what is a governor."[32]

Xenophon himself must have been aware of the real motiva-tions behind Socrates's trial, because he says immediately there-after[33] that Socrates refused to condemn the generals Thrasyllus, Erasinides, and others to death, as requested by the council, on the grounds that such condemnation was illegal. The reference is to an episode when Socrates was presiding over the popular assembly and, as usual, preferred to follow his own conscience rather than common opinion. Some powerful people in Athens never forgave him for his stance. Xenophon then shifts to countering the charge of corrupting youth. He claims that such a charge is obviously ridiculous, given that Socrates was to everyone an example of virtue and temperance:[34] "How, then, should such a man 'corrupt the youth'? Unless, perchance, it be corruption to foster virtue."[35]

Here again one suspects that Xenophon realizes that of course that was precisely the problem: Socrates was telling Athenian youth that the elders of the city, the people in charge, were unvirtuous and unwise. And that truly is "corrupting" youth from the point of view of the establishment! Then again, continues Xenophon, part of the (informal) accusation against Socrates was that some of his associates turned out to be bad for the city, especially two of his students, our old friends Critias and Alcibiades. Xenophon's response here is more than a bit questionable: Those two, he claims, were actually influenced in a positive manner by Socrates while they were associated with him, and it was only after they distanced themselves from the philosopher that they lost their way:

> So long as [Critias and Alcibiades] were with Socrates, they found in him an ally who gave them strength to conquer their evil passions. But when they parted from him, Critias fled to Thessaly, and got among men who put lawlessness before justice; while Alcibiades, on account of his beauty, was hunted by many great ladies, and because of his influence at Athens and among her allies he was spoilt by many powerful men: and as athletes who gain an easy victory in the games are apt to neglect

their training, so the honor in which he was held, the cheap triumph he won with the people, led him to neglect himself.[36]

A better argument—which Xenophon also advances—is that a teacher is not responsible for how all his students turn out: "For what teacher of flute, lyre, or anything else, after making his pupils proficient, is held to blame if they leave him for another master, and then turn out incompetent?"[37]

Xenophon then provides us with a list of Socrates's virtues, beginning with his piety[38] and continuing with his frugality.[39] Here we get some fascinating glimpses of Socrates the practical philosopher, far more than we do from Plato's more consciously intellectual treatment: "He advised those who could not [resist temptation at the dinner table] to avoid appetizers that encouraged them to eat and drink what they did not want: for such trash was the ruin of stomach and brain and soul.... Of sensual passion he would say: 'Avoid it resolutely: it is not easy to control yourself once you meddle with that sort of thing.'"[40]

Xenophon's next move, still part of his overall project of defending Socrates against his accusers, is to remind us that the philosopher was actually critical of the impious. In one episode, Socrates chastises Aristodemus for not sacrificing, praying, or using divination. Socrates explains to Aristodemus why we ought to be convinced that there is a loving god, and the argument he uses is clearly recognizable as an argument from design, still deployed by theists today: "Do you not think then that he who created man from the beginning had some useful end in view when he endowed him with his several senses, giving eyes to see visible objects, ears to hear sounds? Would odors again be of any use to us had we not been endowed with nostrils?... Besides these, are there not other contrivances that look like the result of forethought?... With such signs of forethought in these arrangements, can you doubt whether they are the works of chance or design?"[41]

Note, however, that Socrates often, though not always, refers to God in the singular ("the deity"), as he also typically does in the Platonic dialogues. This is one reason why the charge of impiety might not actually have been that far off the mark. Moreover, Socrates's speech at times becomes downright seditious, as in the following passage, which Xenophon presents as illustrative of Socrates's encouragement of temperance in others: "My friends, if we were at war and wanted to choose a leader most capable of helping us to save ourselves and conquer the enemy, should we choose one whom we knew to be the slave of the belly, or of wine, or lust, or sleep?"[42]

Depending on whom exactly Socrates had in mind when uttering those words, and when and where exactly he uttered them, you could imagine that he made some of the men in power in Athens rather nervous, as they might have recognized themselves in his description of the unvirtuous leader.

Near the end of his defense, and of book I of *Memorabilia*, Xenophon details an illuminating dialogue between the Sophist Antiphon and Socrates, which in part touches on how to better influence the politics of the city. Crucially, at one point, Antiphon remarks that Socrates is in no position to make politicians of others, since he himself has never been a politician. Socrates responds, "How now, Antiphon? Should I play a more important part in politics by engaging in them alone, or by taking pains to turn out as many competent politicians as possible?"[43]

That, in a sense, is precisely one of the chief questions that we are pursuing in this book: How should we increase our chances of acquiring competent and wise political leaders? The next step in our quest will be to take a look at three other case studies from Greco-Roman antiquity along the lines we have already seen. Socrates certainly failed with Alcibiades, but perhaps others fared better. Next up, then, are Socrates's most famous student, Plato, as well as the latter's most successful pupil, Aristotle. We will then jump a few centuries and several hundred miles and examine what happens when a Stoic philosopher, Seneca, attempts to steer a princeps toward virtue.

5

TEACHING VIRTUE TO POLITICIANS

I pondered the matter and was in two minds as to whether I
ought to listen to entreaties and go, or how I ought to act; and
finally the scale turned in favor of the view that, if ever anyone
was to try to carry out in practice my ideas about laws and constitutions, now was the time for making the attempt.

—PLATO, *SEVENTH LETTER*

THERE IS NO WAY AROUND IT: SOCRATES DID NOT SUCCEED IN
his attempt to make Alcibiades into a virtuous statesman,
and the people of Athens paid an irrevocable price for this failure. At least, that's one way to put it. Another is that virtue
can be taught only in the way painting, sculpting, or music can:
There are techniques, yes, and one is well served to find a good
teacher. But ultimately the outcome is determined by the talent and determination of the student. Not even Beethoven can
make you into a decent musician, let alone a great one, if you'd
rather spend your time playing video games.

There are several other examples in ancient Greco-Roman
history of the sort of relationship in which Socrates engaged
with Alcibiades. In order to better grasp the complex nature of
such efforts—the transmission of wisdom from philosopher to

statesman—we will examine three of them in this chapter. Our quest will first move us forward to a few years after Socrates's death. We'll look at Plato's three separate attempts to teach the philosophical way to two tyrants of Syracuse on the island of Sicily. Then we'll consider the tutorship of Alexander the Great by Plato's own student, Aristotle. Finally, we will jump to imperial Rome and scrutinize the fascinating relationship between the Stoic philosopher Seneca and the (allegedly) mad emperor Nero.

These three cases will lead us to a somewhat more nuanced understanding of what happens when a philosopher attempts to instill virtue in a statesman. Each case has similarities with and differences from the story of Socrates and Alcibiades. Let's begin by traveling to the island of Sicily, circa 388 BCE, eleven years after the death of Socrates.

CASE STUDY ONE: PLATO VS. THE TYRANTS

At that time Plato, nearing forty years old, embarked on a series of travels across the Mediterranean that brought him to Egypt, southern Italy, and eventually Syracuse in Sicily—the very city-state that had so dramatically contributed to the defeat of Athens in the Peloponnesian War. In Tarentum, southeastern Italy, Plato met a young and brilliant adviser to the tyrant of Syracuse, Dionysius I. His name was Dion, and he was the son of the Syracusan statesman Hipparinus. His wife was named Arete, which means virtue or excellence. Later, Plato wrote of Dion that he "rapidly assimilated my teaching as he did all forms of knowledge, listened to me with an eagerness which I had never seen equalled in any young man, and resolved to live for the future in a better way than the majority of Italian and

Sicilian Greeks, having set his affection on virtue in preference to pleasure and self-indulgence."[1]

Dion had been interested in intellectual activities since his youth, and he particularly excelled at philosophy. He invited Plato to travel to Syracuse in order to influence Dionysius I, whose court had a reputation for debauchery and definitely little interest in philosophy. In addition, Dionysius I was paranoid about plots to overthrow him. The tyrant agreed to meet the philosopher. Things immediately went south because Dionysius I found Plato's contention that tyranny was the lowest form of government offensive. You see, in the *Republic*, Plato developed a theory that connected the five basic types of government recognized at the time and ranked them from best to worst:[2]

- Aristocracy, rule by the best, meaning the wisest, people. It is the ideal system described in the *Republic*, where the philosophers are kings (obviously).
- Timocracy, the next-best option. Here leaders are chosen not from among the wise but from among the valiant. Sparta was the example par excellence.
- Oligarchy, where the rich (i.e., neither the wise nor the valiant) are in charge and tend to mostly look after their own interests. The modern United States is, practically if not formally, an oligarchic nation.
- Democracy, which at the time meant rule by the simple majority of eligible people (i.e., excluding women and slaves). For Plato, democracy represented the sort of mob rule that dominated Athens and led to the execution of Socrates.
- Tyranny, characterized by a strong man who imposes order at the cost of widespread injustice.

You can imagine how Dionysius I was taken aback at finding his style of leadership at the bottom of the ladder. His reaction, though perhaps predictable, was not lacking in a dark sense of humor. He sold Plato into slavery because, as Plutarch recounts in his biography of Dion, Dionysius said that Plato "would of course take no harm of it, being the same just man as before; he would enjoy that happiness, though he lost his liberty."[3]

Plato was soon rescued by his friends, who paid the ransom for his freedom, and returned to Athens, where he founded his famous Academy. But he wasn't done with Syracuse just yet. Twenty years passed, and Plato was now an elderly man of about sixty. Dionysius I was dead, allegedly poisoned by his successor, Dionysius II, apparently to make sure that he wouldn't at the last minute relinquish his power to Dion. The second Dionysius was an even less promising candidate for a philosopher-king than his father. He had been brought up in isolation so as not to pose a threat to the first Dionysius, which meant he had no experience of politics and holding the reins of power. (Obviously the precaution had not worked.) Moreover, he was even more of a hedonist than his predecessor. Plutarch tells us that at one point, Dionysius II engaged in a ninety-day stretch of drinking, singing, dancing, and buffoonery, utterly refusing to conduct any state business.[4]

The upside of Dionysius II's incompetence and indifference to matters of state was that Dion was effectively in charge of things and again exercised much influence at court. Dion, apparently, was rather optimistic about the chances of steering the young king away from hedonism and toward virtue and began to teach him philosophy. To everyone's astonishment—and to the consternation of the king's close associates—Dionysius II took an interest in philosophical matters, which gave Dion an opening to invite Plato to Syracuse a second time.

The initial effect of Plato's teachings on Dionysius II was remarkable. The king became more sober (literally and metaphorically) and attentive, distancing himself from his court's persistent libertine attitudes. At some point, while conducting a ritual sacrifice, Dionysius II even publicly announced that he wished to step down as tyrant of Syracuse. This announcement did not go over well with his associates, who intensified their plotting to discredit Dion, who was seen as chiefly responsible for the whole damnable state of affairs. Eventually the king listened to his advisers and exiled Dion to Athens while keeping Plato in Syracuse, officially as an esteemed guest but for all effective purposes as a prisoner confined to his admittedly luxurious apartments in the acropolis. In his *Seventh Letter*, Plato describes the complex relationship that developed thereafter: "As time went on, and as intercourse made him acquainted with my disposition and character, he did become more and more attached to me, and wished me to praise him more than I praised Dion.... He shrank from coming into close and intimate relations with me as a pupil and listener to my discourses on philosophy, fearing the danger suggested by mischief-makers, that he might be ensnared."[5]

But even the cautious respect that Dionysius II showed for Plato was not well received at court, where people were fearful of the influence of the philosopher on the king and began to insinuate that Plato had more sinister motives for ingratiating himself with Dionysius. Some went so far as to joke that Syracuse had survived the assault of the Athenian army only to succumb to the stealth conquest of an Athenian philosopher.

Eventually Plato left Syracuse for a second time, though he returned again ten years later, when he was about seventy. One cannot but admire the courage it took to face both multiple perilous journeys at sea and the unstable character of Dionysius, especially for a man in the last years of his life. But Plato was determined not to miss an opportunity to put his theories about statesmanship into practice. Philosophy, even for someone who became known for advancing very esoteric metaphysical notions, is a practical discipline, good only if it changes things on the ground rather than limiting itself to abstract dissertations inside the walls of the Academy.

During this third visit, Plato attempted to mollify Dionysius on behalf of the still exiled Dion. Once again, he failed. Dionysius, however, was compelled by Plato's charisma to resume his philosophical studies, even going so far as to write a book on his mentor's ideas. The book turned out to be full of misunderstandings and plagiarism, but nevertheless, Dionysius did try.

Why did Plato fall flat with the two Dionysiuses? Especially with the second one, who made the mistake of pursuing philosophy as an instrument of power rather than embracing the philosophical way of life and practicing it in his political rule? One might say that Plato failed, but it would be more accurate—just as in the case of Socrates and Alcibiades—to say that it was the student who failed, not the philosopher. Dionysius II could not ascend to the heights where his master dwelled. And his failure, in turn, is understandable once we remember that he had not been exposed to the tools of philosophy during his youth. He did not develop morally in the way required for him to take advantage of Plato's teachings later in his life. In an insightful essay, journalist and author Nick Romeo uses the imagery of Plato's famous allegory of the cave to summarize what happened: The philosopher descended back into the cave in order to help the king emerge from it and see the light of the full reality of things. But the king did not have the moral stamina to climb out and was eventually sucked back into the darkness. Plato was lucky to survive the experience unscathed.

Things did not go much better for Dion, despite his genuine interest in philosophy and the fact that he became one of Plato's best students. He achieved a degree of fame during his exile and was given an honorary citizenship at Sparta. When Dionysius confiscated and sold his estate, pocketing the money, Dion finally rebelled, organizing an expedition of mercenary forces against Syracuse. He largely succeeded, in part thanks to the help of the Carthaginians, Syracuse's great rivals in the southern Mediterranean. Dionysius was deposed, yet he somehow managed to reenter the city and take possession of the acropolis. A bizarre standoff ensued. Dion—now, together with his brother, elected leader of Syracuse—maintained control of much of the city and held off the deposed tyrant, who resisted from inside the fortified citadel. Eventually Dionysius escaped, unharmed.

Dion tried to govern Syracuse justly, but he was an aristocrat who shared Plato's disdain for democracy. This created tension with other local leaders and eventually led to the dissatisfaction of the populace, which triggered his exile. To his credit, Dion could have used his army to stay in Syracuse by force but decided instead to move to the nearby city of Leontini. His adventures were not over yet. Apollocrates, Dionysius's son, had stayed behind in an island fortress, still posing a danger to the recently liberated Syracuse. The Syracusans were unable to dislodge him and called on Dion and his forces for help.

Apollocrates's army left as soon as news of Dion's return began circulating, and Dion entered the city, once again the acclaimed leader. (If you have by now developed a sense that the democratic city-states of ancient Greece were rather fickle in their allegiances to their leaders, you have that right.) Dion then went to work to create as close a lived version of Plato's ideal state as was possible, which entailed establishing an aristocratic Senate, not very different from the one that was at that time presiding over the affairs of the Roman Republic.

In the end, Dion was betrayed by one of his comrades, Calippus, who had accompanied him as part of the original expeditionary force from Greece. Dionysius bribed Calippus to get rid of Dion. On the appointed date, when Dion was at home celebrating a holiday in honor of the goddess Persephone, a group of assassins entered the premises, seized Dion, and stabbed him to death with a short Spartan sword. Predictably, Calippus seized power for himself. And just as predictably, within a year, he faced a revolt that ended with his exile. Syracuse eventually recovered and experienced decades of prosperity under the guidance of Hiero II before falling under Roman control in 212 BCE.

CASE STUDY TWO: ARISTOTLE AND ALEXANDER

Alexander III of Macedon, commonly referred to as "the Great," was for three years an eager and brilliant student of Aristotle of Stagira, himself a student of Plato. As Michael Tierney writes in a classic essay on the topic, there are several excellent reasons to study the fourth century BCE, and the working relationship between two such extraordinary men as Alexander and Aristotle ranks high among such reasons.

The action takes place just twelve years after Plato's final failure at Syracuse. He died in 348/347 BCE, at about age eighty, and Speusippus inherited the leading role at the Academy. Unfortunately, Speusippus evidently was not up to the task, which caused a split among Plato's pupils. Aristotle was one of a number who left Athens, crossed the Aegean Sea, and ended up in Assos, near Troy (in modern western Turkey). Several former members of the Academy worked there under the patronage of Hermias of Atarneus, who happened to be a close friend of King Philip of Macedon, Alexander's father. Aristotle had another close connection with the royal family, as his father had been the personal physician of Amyntas, Philip's father. Moreover, Aristotle became a close friend of Hermias and ended up marrying the latter's adopted daughter.

During three intense years at Assos, Aristotle carried out much of his work on biology, which he then continued at Mytilene, on the island of Lesbos. But he was soon interrupted, summoned to the court of Philip, and charged with tutoring the then thirteen-year-old Alexander. Aristotle taught his pupil until 340 BCE, when the youth became regent in Macedon at age sixteen and took the field with his army. Just four years later, Philip was assassinated and Alexander succeeded to the throne, beginning the most ambitious geopolitical and military project the Western world had ever seen. This project would continue—in different forms—even after Alexander's premature death at age thirty-three, leaving to his lieutenants a vast empire stretching from Greece to Egypt and from Mesopotamia to Persia.

When Aristotle was given charge of Alexander, he was not the world-renowned philosopher he would later become, but he was certainly an established scholar, aged forty, with a number of influential books already in his name, including his personal manifesto, *De Philosophia*. He would soon write the *Politics*, which scholars maintain influenced Alexander during his early campaigns, before his thinking began to diverge significantly from that of his mentor. Just as importantly, Aristotle gave

Alexander a personally annotated version of Homer's *Iliad*, by which the young prince was so strongly influenced that he later always brought it with him during his campaigns, as Plutarch writes: "He was naturally a great lover of all kinds of learning and reading; and Onesicritus informs us that he constantly laid Homer's Iliad, according to the copy corrected by Aristotle, called the casket copy, with his dagger under his pillow, declaring that he esteemed it a perfect portable treasure of all military virtue and knowledge."[6]

Alexander even claimed descent—on his mother's side—from the Achaean hero Achilles, and when he started his "Greek war of revenge" against the Persians, he made a point of visiting Troy. Just as telling of Alexander's character is his claim that—on his father's side—he was descended from Heracles, the demigod who would become a role model for both Cynic and Stoic philosophers during the Hellenistic era.

Plutarch tells us that Alexander was instructed by Aristotle in the philosopher's doctrines of morals and politics as well as in "those more abstruse and profound theories which these philosophers, by the very names they gave them, professed to reserve for oral communication to the initiated, and did not allow many to become acquainted with."[7] We don't know exactly what Plutarch is referring to here, but it is fascinating that Aristotle is known for having written two entirely different types of works, one "exoteric," aimed at a general public, and one "esoteric," reserved for his students at the Lyceum. Only the esoteric works survive, in the form of lecture notes, which makes Aristotle difficult for the modern reader to approach. We have testimony from antiquity that, by contrast, the exoteric works were beautifully written and accessible. Cicero, in his *Academica*, goes so far as to say that Aristotle, in those works, poured a "river of gold." It is highly unfortunate that we no longer have access to such writings.

Apparently Alexander was appreciative and even somewhat protective of the teachings he received from his mentor. So much so that he was not happy when Aristotle later published some of the material he had used to instruct the young prince. Alexander complained in a letter to his mentor:[8]

> Alexander to Aristotle, greeting.
> You have not done well to publish your books of oral doctrine; for what is there now that we excel others in, if those things which we have been particularly instructed in be laid open to all? For my part, I assure you, I had rather excel others in the knowledge of what is excellent, than in the extent of my power and dominion.
>
> Farewell.

Despite this somewhat peevish reaction, Alexander was fond of Aristotle, saying that he considered him a second father. While Philip gave him life, Aristotle taught him how to live as well as how to appreciate and preserve knowledge.

Alexander always brought a number of scholars on his expeditions so that new knowledge could be acquired and cataloged. He founded new cities with repositories for such knowledge, and he even gave Aristotle himself a grant—as we would call it today—of eight hundred talents to continue pursuing his research in natural philosophy. This attitude survived Alexander: One chunk of his empire, in Egypt, came under the control of what is known as the Ptolemy dynasty, and it was Ptolemy I who commissioned the creation of the legendary Library of Alexandria. That commission was a concrete step toward realizing

Alexander's dream of housing the output of all human creative activities in a single place—naturally named after himself.

Even more relevant to the project of this book are Aristotle's and Alexander's respective conceptions of politics and how to practice it. Naturally Aristotle initially greatly influenced Alexander in this area. However, the conqueror's views eventually diverged sharply from those of the philosopher. In order to grasp the evolution of Alexander's political thought, we need to step back and see how Aristotle perceived his pupil, especially given Aristotle's awareness of Plato's failures with the two Dionysiuses. Aristotle thought that a good and influential man (he definitely was concerned only with men) had to have three characteristics: physis (nature), ethos (education), and logos (intellect). Alexander seemed to fit the ideal very well. He was naturally disposed to learning, having demonstrated readiness to acknowledge his mistakes and to acquire knowledge from others. He was inclined toward practical wisdom, realizing that action needs to be guided by good judgment. Finally, his intellect proved sharper than most others in the ancient world. He was, therefore, an excellent candidate for the role of philosopher-king.

Aristotle thought the whole point of ruling was to lead one's people to flourish, and this could be accomplished only by a ruler who had both a good character and the wisdom to navigate the complexities of the world. Plutarch certainly thought that Alexander fit the bill, comparing him to two of the great Athenian statesmen: Pericles in terms of political skill and Themistocles in terms of practical wisdom.[9] (Nota bene, *not* to Alcibiades!) Alexander himself was well aware of what he was doing and why, remarking, again according to Plutarch, that he received more assistance from the teachings of Aristotle than from the armies that he inherited from his father.[10]

How did Alexander go about implementing his political vision? Again, he initially followed the theory and inspiration of his teacher. According to Aristotle, the human animal is a political one, meaning in part that it does not just live but thrives in a polis, a city. It is therefore not at all surprising that Alexander engaged in a frantic program of city building wherever he went and conquered. By some accounts, he founded fifty cities named after himself, the most famous being the one in Egypt (yes, he certainly was more than a bit narcissistic). The Alexandrian cities were meant as a practical implementation of the Aristotelian idea: They were centers of civil society where the arts and sciences flourished and where good communal living was the entire purpose of the enterprise. Yet these cities were not meant to act as the Greek city-states had acted throughout much of their history, as each other's rivals and enemies. Rather, the idea was to promote universal well-being, with each city acting as a friend to all the others, a friendship made possible by a commonality of law and education across the world. Plutarch comments that Alexander was trying to create not an empire but rather a global polis based on mutual friendship and characterized by general flourishing. Of course he went about it in the only way that was conceivable in his time: by imposing his vision by force whenever it wasn't possible to persuade people by reason.

It is precisely when we consider Alexander's vision of globalization—to use a modern term—that his ideas begin to diverge sharply from those of Aristotle. Let us start with Aristotle's view, which was shaped by the Greek experience before, during, and after the Persian Wars. Before the Persians invaded Hellas, the Greeks were already very much aware of their common cultural heritage but did not contemplate any kind of political union. The arrival of the Persians, who threatened to subjugate the independent city-states, forged the first Panhellenic political alliance, initially under the guidance of Sparta and then under that of Athens.

The Athenian rhetorician Isocrates is usually credited as the first to expressly articulate, in his *Panegyricus*, a Panhellenic vision based not just on common ancestry but on a shared culture (the Athenian one, of course). Aristotle, however, is the one who developed this view and attempted to put it into practice by way of his influence on Alexander. Aristotle still did not conceive of Panhellenism as a political unity; in fact, he saw the project as compatible with the existence of city-states characterized by different systems of government. As Andrey Kortunov points out in his brilliant essay on Aristotle and Alexander, think of something like a European Union *ante litteram*, sans so much insistence on democracy.

Aristotle was a complex character, in some respects remarkably open-minded. He opposed all forms of tyranny, defended human rights (although "human" didn't include women and slaves), and admired whatever was to be admired in different populations of "barbarians," including the Egyptians, the Persians, and the Scythians. At the same time, in the *Politics*, he wrote that northern Europeans are courageous yet not very bright on account of the cold climate. By contrast, Asians (meaning Persians) are smart and cultivate the arts but lack courage. It will come as no surprise that the happy middle ground (Aristotle was always looking for a happy medium!) is represented by the Greeks, who live in intermediate climates and combine the best of the barbarians' attributes. That is why, according to Aristotle, the Greeks were free and their cities were characterized by the best governments. Moreover, Aristotle believed that the Greeks could have ruled the world if they had gotten their act together and developed a unified policy. We could call it Greek exceptionalism, to paraphrase Kortunov, in the same way that we nowadays talk about the idea of American exceptionalism.

Alexander at first modeled his policy on Aristotle's thought but eventually dramatically transcended the scope of his master's project, a true case of the pupil surpassing the teacher, at least in ambition. Let's return to our story and see how this evolved.

After Alexander's father, Philip of Macedon, had essentially established control over all of Greece, Alexander developed the notion of a "war of revenge" against the Persians, in part as a convenient excuse to march his army east and in part to unify the Greeks behind his banner. It was yet another attempt at national unity by way of a common enemy, only this time it was the Greeks who threatened the Persian empire rather than the other way around. There is no reason to doubt that Alexander's political ambitions were initially inspired by the very same Pan-hellenic sentiment that was articulated by both Isocrates and Aristotle. But as Alexander's conquest of the known world progressed, and as he came into direct contact with other cultures, he began to outgrow that limited Panhellenic perspective. In essence, Alexander ultimately developed the first truly cosmo-politan political program of antiquity.

Arguably the turning point was marked by some of Alexander's early victories against Darius III, the Persian king. After Alexander defeated the Persians at both Granicus (334 BCE) and Issus (333 BCE), Darius presented Alexander with a generous offer: Split the Persian territory along the River Euphrates and call it even. That would have been an incredible achievement for the young Macedonian king and would have, for all effective purposes, made Darius his junior partner in Asia. At home, Alexander would have been hailed as the uncontested ruler of all of Greece. Aristotle would likely have been pleased with such an outcome.

But Alexander rejected Darius's offer and continued his march forward to fight and win in Persia and all the way to India. While his project was pursued through war and the inevitable violence of conquest, Alexander as ruler proved to be remarkably tolerant of cultural and religious diversity wherever he went, from Egypt to India. He embraced local customs and tried to forge a syncretic path forward whereby Greek culture would enrich Egypt, Persia, and other places in the world but would also be enriched in turn—a notion that would have been anathema to Aristotle. Alexander's political vision had now grown well beyond Panhellenism, as attested by his choosing Babylon as the administrative center of his empire. His political vision had morphed into a uniquely cosmopolitan one.

Alexander was complicated at a personal level, and his complex character determined his military and political actions. It is just as reasonable to see him as a despot as to see him as an enlightened ruler. He certainly was generous with his friends and enjoyed a lavish party. At the same time, he seems to have been personally rather indifferent to material wealth. His project of conquest appears to have been motivated by a genuine desire to make the world a better place, a notion that he vigorously pursued not just by way of his formidable army but by mass weddings between his associates (and himself) and locals, the encouragement of migration from one part of the empire to another, and his ecumenical approach to religion, welcoming all sorts of local gods into a preview of the equally politically and socially effective Roman pantheon. Plutarch perhaps puts it best: "[He] did not, as Aristotle advised him, rule the Grecians like a moderate prince and insult over the barbarians like an absolute tyrant.... Believing himself sent from Heaven as the common moderator and arbiter of all nations, and subduing those by force whom he could not associate to himself by fair offers, he labored thus, that he might bring all regions, far and near, under the same dominion. And then, as in a festival goblet, mixing lives, manners, customs, wedlock, all together, he ordained that everyone should take the whole habitable world for his country."[11]

Modern sensibilities will rightly object to a cosmopolitan project forged by invading armies, but we don't know how things might have turned out had Alexander lived longer than his thirty-three years. Even though he hadn't had enough time to consolidate his vision by the time he died, and even though his empire would eventually be split into several sizable chunks (Egypt, Syria, Greece-Macedon, etc.) and later be absorbed by the expanding power of Rome, Alexander's united vision of a cosmopolitanism originally inspired by the philosophical ideals of Hellenism took root on three continents and continues to be influential to this day. Aristotle's project, by comparison, appears small, parochial, and more than a bit snobbish. Over two millennia later, we still aspire to a unified humanity that thrives on cultural diversity, a world where local polities work in harmony with other such polities to confront global problems and to foster the flourishing of their citizens. That, ultimately, was Alexander's vision, and we are still looking for new ways to pursue it.

CASE STUDY THREE: SENECA AND NERO

Our third case study of relationships between a philosopher and a statesman in Greco-Roman antiquity is the famous, or infamous, one featuring Seneca and Nero. Nero was a Roman emperor who has often been characterized as a monster but according to other sources has historically been a victim of unjust vilification. Meanwhile, Seneca's reputation as a politician, a businessman, and a philosopher is, shall we say, mixed, although nobody disputes the influence of his Latin tragedies on modern theater, most significantly his influence on William Shakespeare. Seneca was indubitably sexist, unarguably failed to rein in Nero, and possibly (though unwittingly) triggered the bloody Boudican rebellion in Britannia by suddenly calling in a vast amount of loans he had made to the local aristocracy.

Even Seneca's physical appearance has been a matter of dispute for quite some time, reflecting the ambiguity of commentators' assessment of him as a man. For centuries, he was portrayed as emaciated, but we now know—from a double herm preserved at the Pergamon Museum in Berlin that represents him, interestingly, opposite Socrates—that he was actually a bit plump. The scrawnier version known as pseudo-Seneca, now suspected of actually representing either the playwright Aristophanes or the poet Hesiod, was more appealing because it simply fit better with the idea of the philosopher-sage lost in thought and unconcerned with worldly goods, while the Pergamon version smacks of a well-fed patrician who may have been talking the Stoic talk but not walking the Stoic walk.

Seneca's figure is so fascinating that two full modern biographies of him have been published, both well worth reading: *The Greatest Empire*, by Emily Wilson, and *Dying Every Day*, by James Romm. And that's without counting the 1920 classic *The Stoic*, by Francis Caldwell Holland. Clearly there is a wealth of material to dig into for people interested in Seneca as a historical figure. Not to mention his many extant works, including

THE MAJOR EVENTS IN THE SENECA-NERO TIMELINE

- 4 BCE: Seneca is born in Corduba, modern Spain.
- 37 CE: Nero is born in Antium, just south of Rome.
- 41 CE: Seneca is sent into exile to Corsica.
- 49 CE: Seneca is recalled to Rome by Agrippina, Claudius's fourth wife and Nero's mother.
- 54 CE: Nero ascends to the throne at age seventeen after the death of the emperor Claudius, who was possibly poisoned by Agrippina.
- 54–62 CE: Seneca acts as Nero's adviser in collaboration with the praetorian prefect Sextus Afranius Burrus.
- 55 CE: Britannicus (son of Claudius and the former empress Messalina) is poisoned, almost certainly on Nero's order; the death eliminates a possible future competitor for Nero and is probably triggered by Agrippina's threat to Nero to switch her allegiance to Britannicus.
- 58 CE: Agrippina is murdered on Nero's orders, possibly in response to her participation in a conspiracy and certainly because of her repeated attempts to assert influence and power.
- 55–60 CE: Nero takes on the role of consul four times in this period, and several ancient historians—as well as the emperor Trajan—speak well of his principate at this point, in contrast with his later rule.
- 62–64 CE: Seneca tries to retire twice and is twice rebuffed by Nero.
- 64 CE: Nero is accused of setting the great fire of Rome and even of playing the lyre while watching his city burn. In reality, he was outside Rome and poured a lot of effort and resources into rebuilding the devastated area.
- 65 CE: Gaius Calpurnius Piso organizes a conspiracy against Nero, which fails.
- 65 CE: Nero suspects Seneca of being part of the Pisonian conspiracy and orders him to commit suicide. Seneca was likely not an active party in the plot but just as likely knew of it and did not alert the emperor.
- 68 CE: Having become increasingly erratic and paranoid, Nero commits suicide or has one of his trusted men kill him. The Julio-Claudian dynasty comes to an end, chaos ensues, and things eventually settle down again with the advent of the emperor Vespasian.

plays, letters of consolation, philosophical essays, and letters to his friend Lucilius.

What can we glimpse from this wealth of historical material? To begin with, it is true that Seneca was very wealthy, indeed one of the wealthiest and most influential men in Rome. That in and of itself, however, does not constitute a contradiction with his Stoic philosophy. For the Stoics, wealth falls into the category of what they call "preferred indifferents," that is, the sort of things that it is okay to pursue so long as they don't get in the way of the only thing that truly matters for a Stoic: the improvement of one's character. Then again, Seneca repeatedly warns about the many temptations induced by wealth, almost as a reminder to himself: "He who craves riches feels fear on their account. No man, however, enjoys a blessing that brings anxiety; he is always trying to add a little more. While he puzzles over increasing his wealth, he forgets how to use it. He collects his accounts, he wears out the pavement in the forum, he turns over his ledger—in short, he ceases to be master and becomes a steward."[12]

Seneca experienced a number of highs and lows in his life. When he was in his midforties, he lost a great deal of his wealth, and in 41 CE, he was exiled by the Senate on a likely trumped-up charge of committing adultery with Julia Livilla, the sister of the former emperor Caligula—the guy who made his favorite horse a senator. The new emperor, Claudius, commuted the original death penalty to exile, and the historian Cassius Dio suggests that Seneca was a victim of an attempt by Messalina, Claudius's wife, to get rid of Julia. Seneca remained in exile on the island of Corsica (at the time not at all the resort destination that it is today) for eight years.

After Claudius's death, Seneca penned an essay of dubious taste, known as "On the Pumpkinification of the Divine

Claudius," where he mocks an emperor who, after all, had spared his life (and whom he had flattered in order to obtain a pardon), all the while attempting to ingratiate himself with the new kid on the block, Nero, whose mother, Agrippina, had managed to recall Seneca from exile. Definitely questionable behavior for a good Stoic. Then again, even regarding this episode, there is a variety of opinions. Here, for instance, is Allan Presley Ball, who translated the Pumpkinification essay: "Seneca appears also to have been concerned with what he saw as an overuse of apotheosis writing as a political tool. [Apotheosis was the process by which dead Roman emperors were recognized as gods.] If an Emperor as flawed as Claudius could receive such treatment, [Seneca] argued elsewhere, then people would cease to believe in the gods at all."[13]

Concerning the abovementioned calling in of loans that allegedly caused the rebellion in the British provinces, it is actually far from clear whether Seneca's actions were a contributing factor and even more doubtful that he was aware of the risk when he made the decision on financial grounds. Also, regarding wealth, Seneca apparently wasn't particularly attached to his considerable holdings. In fact, once things began to go south with Nero, he tried to use his financial means to buy himself retirement and to dedicate his time to philosophy. The attempt succeeded only partially (he got to spend more time at one of his country estates) and only temporarily, until Nero ordered Seneca to commit suicide.

Seneca's use of his wealth, however, may have been most important—and also most difficult to disentangle from his political intentions and actions—during the first five years of Nero's reign. During that period, the philosopher advised the young emperor in coordination with the praetorian prefect Sextus

Afranius Burrus. Those years, according to most historians, were actually prosperous for Rome, so we can legitimately infer that Seneca and Burrus did a good job under very precarious and difficult circumstances.

In time, Nero became increasingly paranoid (sometimes for good reasons, since there actually were plots against his life) and eventually murdered his own mother, Agrippina—the same person who had persuaded Claudius to recall Seneca from exile. Seneca and Burrus likely had nothing to do with Agrippina's murder, since their influence on Nero was by then already on the wane. It is, however, definitely the case that Seneca wrote a speech for the Senate essentially excusing the murder. While writing such a speech is surely not in line with Stoic principles and in fact is simply highly objectionable on general moral grounds, it is impossible to know exactly what was going on in Seneca's mind. He may, for instance, have calculated that by way of this move, he would be able to rein in and steer Nero, thus saving Rome from a tyrant or yet another bloody civil war. If that was his plan, it failed. Three years later, Burrus died, which further escalated the situation, eventually leading to the Pisonian conspiracy and consequently to Seneca's own death. Whatever his political mistakes, he paid for them with his life.

Regarding Seneca's mandated suicide, unsympathetic commentators claim that he staged things in order to appear as a Roman Socrates. If this is true, however, the plan didn't go smoothly. It took him several attempts to finally comply with the emperor's order. The accusations, though, seem more than a bit uncharitable, as he did die unjustly. While Seneca surely had Socrates, a role model for Stoics, in mind, he was likely trying to do his best while performing the last act of his life, so let's cut the guy some slack.

When taking an overall look at Seneca's political influence and his behavior with Nero, we need to remember a couple of things. To begin with, we have only a few contemporary or near contemporary accounts of what happened, mostly from people who clearly and openly disliked Seneca. Moreover, controlling a sociopathic tyrant is a task not many would even attempt, let alone succeed at, so perhaps we shouldn't be too surprised that Seneca was able to handle Nero for only a few years.

Seneca's reputation has always experienced rather dramatic ups and downs, from his own time until now. The Roman historian Tacitus claims in *The Annals of Imperial Rome* that accusations against Seneca did not hold up to scrutiny and were likely the result of envy or political antagonism. The early Christian fathers thought highly of Seneca, with Tertullian referring to him as "our Seneca." In *The Divine Comedy*, Dante puts Seneca in Limbo rather than the depths of Hell—a high honor for a pagan. (We should note, however, that another Stoic, Cato the Younger, receives an even higher honor with his placement at the entrance of Purgatory. In Dante's words, "What man on earth was more worthy to signify God than Cato? Surely none." We'll encounter Cato in the next chapter.) Several pre-Renaissance and Renaissance authors, including Chaucer, Petrarch, Erasmus, John of Salisbury, and Montaigne, celebrated Seneca as a writer and philosopher.

In modern times, Anna Lydia Motto challenges the nowadays common negative portrait of Seneca, which she points out is based almost entirely on the account of Publius Suillius Rufus, a senatorial lieutenant who served under Claudius: "We are therefore left with no contemporary record of Seneca's life, save for the desperate opinion of Publius Suillius. Think of the barren image we should have of Socrates, had the works of Plato and

Xenophon not come down to us and were we wholly dependent upon Aristophanes' description of this Athenian philosopher. To be sure, we should have a highly distorted, misconstrued view. Such is the view left to us of Seneca, if we were to rely upon Suillius alone."[14]

Philosopher Martha Nussbaum maintains that Seneca's intellectual contributions are significantly more original than was previously thought, on topics ranging from the role played by emotions in our lives[15] to political philosophy to his concept of cosmopolitanism.[16] Another contemporary scholar, Robert Wagoner, wrote about the complex question of the relationship between Seneca's life and his philosophy, "Perhaps Seneca simply fails to live the philosophical life he aspires to live. Perhaps his philosophical ambitions were really secondary to his political ambitions. While many scholars have noted the inconsistencies and many have rejected Seneca's work on the grounds of hypocrisy, some scholars (notably Emily Wilson) have challenged this view. Wilson notes that, 'The most interesting question is not why Seneca failed to practice what he preached, but why he preached what he did, so adamantly and so effectively, given the life he found himself leading.'"[17]

We could, of course, also ask the man himself. And this is what he has to say:

> What, then, am I myself doing with my leisure? I am trying to cure my own sores. If I were to show you a swollen foot, or an inflamed hand, or some shriveled sinews in a withered leg, you would permit me to lie quiet in one place and to apply lotions to the diseased member. But my trouble is greater than any of these, and I cannot show it to you. The abscess, or ulcer, is deep within my breast. Pray, pray, do not commend me, do not say:

'What a great man! He has learned to despise all things; condemning the madnesses of man's life, he has made his escape!'
I have condemned nothing except myself. There is no reason
why you should desire to come to me for the sake of making
progress. You are mistaken if you think that you will get any
assistance from this quarter; it is not a physician that dwells
here, but a sick man. I would rather have you say, on leaving
my presence: 'I used to think him a happy man and a learned
one, and I had pricked up my ears to hear him; but I have been
defrauded. I have seen nothing, heard nothing which I craved
and which I came back to hear.' If you feel thus, and speak thus,
some progress has been made. I prefer you to pardon rather
than envy my retirement.[18]

At the very least, he appears to be humble and to have learned
something from critically reflecting on his own life. But there is
a particular piece of writing by Seneca that is very germane to
our understanding of his relationship with Nero, and especially
how Seneca attempted to balance his role as a statesman and
a philosopher: the treatise known as *On Clemency*, written in
55–56 CE and addressed to the then young emperor, aiming to
influence the tone of the latter's principate from the beginning.
It is also a subtle attempt to influence the young princeps's character and steer him toward the exercise of justice.

On Clemency is a study contrasting the good ruler with the
tyrant, obviously written to nudge Nero to practice virtue as the
mark of an enlightened sovereign. It begins with Seneca openly
stating the purpose of the treatise: "I have determined to write a
book upon clemency, Nero Caesar, in order that I may as it were
serve as a mirror to you, and let you see yourself. . . . It is worth
your while to consider and investigate a good conscience from

every point of view, and afterwards to cast your eyes upon this enormous mass of mankind—quarrelsome, factious, and passionate as they are."[19]

To hold oneself as someone else's mirror is what Aristotle says true friends do for each other, and it is one of our most effective ways to keep our path on the side of virtue. Shortly afterward, Seneca both flatters Nero and subtly reminds him of his good character lest he forget it now that he is in power: "The Roman people were in a state of great hazard as long as it was uncertain how your generous disposition would turn out; now, however, the prayers of the community are sure of an answer, for there is no fear that you should suddenly forget your own character."[20]

Note the reference to the "uncertainty" of the Roman people, after which Seneca explains to Nero what clemency is and why it is a good thing to practice: "There are some who imagine that clemency only saves the life of every villain, because clemency is useless except after conviction, and alone of all the virtues has no function among the innocent.... [Yet] clemency not only succors the innocent, but often the virtuous, since in the course of time it happens that men are punished for actions which deserve praise."[21]

Seneca reminds Nero that people are willing to subject themselves to great sacrifices, including going to war, if they consider their sovereign to be just. This and other not-so-subtle warnings to Nero are scattered throughout the text. Seneca elaborates by introducing a metaphor of the head of state as the "soul" to the "body" represented by the people, from which he derives the following: "If, as we may infer from what has been said, you are the soul of the state, and the state is your body, you will perceive, I imagine, how necessary clemency is; for when you appear to spare another, you are really sparing yourself."[22]

Clemency, that is, happens to be in the interest of the ruler himself. Then comes another warning: "A cruel reign is disordered and hidden in darkness, and while all shake with terror at the sudden explosions, not even he who caused all this disturbance escapes unharmed."[23] Here, "he who caused all this disturbance" is none other than the emperor himself, of course. And again: "The safety of kings on the other hand is more surely founded on kindness, because frequent punishment may crush the hatred of a few, but excites that of all."[24]

At this point, Seneca evokes Octavian Augustus—the first Roman emperor—as a model of the benign sovereign, a model Nero would do well to study and follow. And after the carrot comes the stick: "Clemency, then, makes princes safer as well as more respected, and is a glory to empires besides being their most trustworthy means of preservation.... What is the difference between the tyrant and the king—for their outward symbols of authority and their powers are the same—except it be that tyrants take delight in cruelty, whereas kings are only cruel for good reasons and because they cannot help it."[25]

And just in case Nero didn't get the message: "No courage is so great as that which is born of utter desperation. In order to keep people down by terror, you must grant them a certain amount of security, and let them see that they have far more to hope for than to fear: for otherwise, if a man is in equal peril whether he sits still or takes action, he will feel actual pleasure in risking his life, and will fling it away as lightly as though it were not his own."[26]

Two more along the same lines: "Cruel punishments do a king no honor: for who doubts that he is able to inflict them? But, on the other hand, it does him great honor to restrain his powers, to save many from the wrath of others, and sacrifice no one to his own"[27] and "There is no more noble spectacle than that of a sovereign who has received an injury without avenging it."[28]

The philosopher then adds a reminder to Nero about what the purpose of punishment actually is: "Let us now pass on to the consideration of wrongs done to others, in avenging which the law has aimed at three ends, which the prince will do well to aim at also: they are, either that it may correct him whom it punishes, or that his punishment may render other men better, or that, by bad men being put out of the way, the rest may live without fear."[29]

Nowhere is there any room for personal vengeance by the emperor or cruelty to his enemies. Indeed, cruelty is a disease: "This accursed disease of the mind reaches its highest pitch of madness when cruelty itself turns into pleasure, and the act of killing a man becomes enjoyment. Such a ruler is soon cast down from his throne; his life is attempted by poison one day and by the sword the next; he is exposed to as many dangers as there are men to whom he is dangerous."[30] Seneca at this point turns almost prophetical: "Sometimes their own guards have risen in revolt, and have used against their master all the deceit, disloyalty, and ferocity which they have learned from him. What, indeed, can he expect from those whom he has taught to be wicked?"[31]

Finally, we find an explicit defense of Stoicism, Seneca's own chosen philosophy, accompanied by the implicit suggestion that Nero should regard that practice as an inspiration for his own conduct: "Thus the wise man will not pity men, but will help them and be of service to them, seeing that he is born to be a help to all men and a public benefit, of which he will bestow a share upon every one.... Whenever he is able he will interpose between Fortune and her victims: for what better employment can he find for his wealth or his strength than in setting up again what chance has overthrown?"[32]

All of the above quotations reinforce the view commonly held by a number of historians that Seneca tried to guide and rein in Nero amid clear signs of the emperor's unstable character and succeeded, for a time. In this light, even Seneca's infamous speech justifying Agrippina's murder may be seen as a last-ditch attempt to manage a situation that was rapidly getting out of control. Let's not forget that Agrippina did conspire against Nero, repeatedly. She was no innocent soul caught in the storm and likely had in fact murdered her husband, Claudius.

Seneca was most certainly not a sage, but he set himself a task arguably more difficult than the one Socrates had with Alcibiades, who after all was no absolute tyrant of Athens. Nor was this a case of Aristotle attempting to influence a brilliant and eager Alexander. The situation was, if anything, closer to the pickle Plato got himself into with the two Dionysiuses. The difference is that Plato escaped with his life, while Seneca was not so fortunate.

So can politicians be taught? In these three episodes, we have closely observed the challenges each philosopher faced: one in Athens, one in Macedonia, and finally one in imperial Rome. Importantly, we can also see the possibilities offered by each situation for a philosophical project that could aid and inform a statesman and, therefore, benefit the whole of society. What happens, then, if the statesman himself is inclined toward philosophy, embracing it most willingly as a guide for his life and policies? We'll examine three such cases in the next chapter.

6

PHILOSOPHER-KINGS, ANYONE?

As for our friend Cato, you do not love him more than I do:
but after all, with the very best intentions and the most absolute
honesty, he sometimes does harm to the Republic. He speaks
and votes as though he were in the Republic of Plato, not in the
scum of Romulus.

—Cicero, *Letters to Atticus*, 2.1.8

WE HAVE SEEN THE PERILS AND TRIBULATIONS THAT HAVE
accompanied various cases of philosophers attempting
to teach virtue to politicians and statesmen. Perhaps, then, as
Plato suggested in the *Republic*, we should entrust the guidance of our polities to philosophers instead. I know what you
are thinking: How predictable! A philosopher who tells us that
members of his profession just happen to be the best for the
job! The objection is reasonable, but we need to understand
that "philosopher" here most certainly does not mean someone
with a PhD in philosophy who holds an academic post—such
as yours truly. "Philosophers" are those who wish to practice the
art of living, strive to become the best human beings they can
be, and emphasize their deeds, not just their words.

As strange as it may sound nowadays, the two meanings of "philosopher"—the inquirer into the nature of reality and the person who attempts to live wisely—have coexisted from the beginning, and not just in the Western tradition. Buddha, Confucius, and Lao Tzu were nothing if not practical philosophers in ancient India and China, just as Socrates was in ancient Athens. Within the Western tradition, however, there is a sharp distinction between the two meanings of the word "philosophy," and the line of demarcation begins precisely with Socrates. There is a reason that we speak of "Presocratic" philosophers, such as Thales, Anaximander, Anaximenes, Parmenides, and Heraclitus, who were concerned mostly with metaphysics and natural philosophy, that is, what we would today largely regard as science. Socrates was one of the first to explicitly turn away from such concerns on the (then reasonable!) ground that not much progress could be made in that department anyway. Instead, he focused on human issues, ethics (how to conduct one's life), politics (how to run human societies), and epistemology (how humans come to know things).

It is Socrates himself who explains what happened in the *Phaedo*, a Platonic dialogue dedicated to the subject of the immortality of the soul. It is the fourth and last dialogue of the tetralogy concerned with Socrates's trial and execution (the others are *Euthyphro*, *Apology*, and *Crito*). The scene is set in the prison where Socrates waits to drink the hemlock, and it is the last day of his life. Naturally he is engaged in a deep philosophical conversation with a group of friends, including two visitors from Thebes, Cebes and Simmias. At some point in the conversation, Socrates explains his own evolution as a philosopher to Cebes:

When I was young, Cebes, I had a prodigious desire to know that department of philosophy which is called the investigation of nature [i.e., science]; to know the causes of things, and why a thing is and is created or destroyed appeared to me to be a lofty profession. What expectations I had formed, and how grievously was I disappointed! As I proceeded, I found my philosopher [Parmenides] altogether forsaking mind or any other principle of order, but having recourse to air, and ether, and water, and other eccentricities. I might compare him to a person who began by maintaining generally that mind is the cause of the actions of Socrates, but who, when he endeavored to explain the causes of my several actions in detail, went on to show that I sit here because my body is made up of bones and muscles; and the bones, as he would say, are hard and have joints which divide them, and the muscles are elastic, and they cover the bones, which have also a covering or environment of flesh and skin which contains them; and as the bones are lifted at their joints by the contraction or relaxation of the muscles, I am able to bend my limbs, and this is why I am sitting here in a curved posture—that is what he would say, and he would have a similar explanation of my talking to you, which he would attribute to sound, and air, and hearing, and he would assign ten thousand other causes of the same sort, forgetting to mention the true cause, which is, that the Athenians have thought fit to condemn me, and accordingly I have thought it better and more right to remain here and undergo my sentence.[1]

What Socrates says, in effect, is that Parmenides & Co. talk about lofty things of which they cannot possibly know much. And, more crucially, they miss the important point: understanding and improving human actions.

This distinction between philosophy as theoretical inquiry and philosophy as a way of life has perhaps never been sharper than in our current era. If you wonder what the meaning of life is, or how to become a better person, I strongly advise you against walking into an academic philosophy department. You will likely be greeted with dumbfounded looks, if not overt scorn. Indeed, some solid empirical research has been done on the connection between theory and practice in modern academic philosophy, and it turns out that moral philosophers are not an ounce more moral than other academics.[2] This sort of finding would puzzle Socrates. He might even conclude that his modern colleagues are a bunch of Sophists, or at the very least philosophers with their heads sadly in the clouds.

One of the first modern authors to attempt to again draw attention to the importance of philosophy as the art of living was the French scholar Pierre Hadot, especially in his *Philosophy as a Way of Life—Spiritual Exercises from Socrates to Foucault*, published in 1995. In that book, Hadot wasn't concerned particularly with philosopher-kings, though he did write another volume presenting us with a superb commentary on Marcus Aurelius. Rather, he thought that philosophy should guide every thinking person's life. If so, this should be even more true in the case of those among us who wish to take upon themselves the burden of leading the rest. In this chapter, we'll examine the lives and characters of three such examples from antiquity: the Roman senator and statesman Cato the Younger and two rare instances of actual philosopher-kings: Marcus Aurelius and Julian of Constantinople, known as the Apostate.

CASE STUDY ONE: THE CATO CHRONICLES

Cato the Younger, also known as Cato Uticensis, is the quintessential Stoic role model, arguably second only to Socrates among people who actually existed (the Stoics also referred to mythological role models such as Odysseus). Seneca—whom we encountered in the previous chapter—famously cites Cato a number of times throughout his writings. For instance, "Cato will bear with an equally stout heart anything that thwarts him of his victory, as he bore that which thwarted him of his prae-torship. The day whereon he failed of election, he spent in play; the night wherein he intended to die, he spent in reading."[3] One wishes more modern politicians would spend the day they lose the election harmlessly playing with their friends.

Cato became a legendary figure in Roman history, an ex-ample of absolute character integrity. A decidedly apocryphal story, recounted by Plutarch, gives us an idea of the regard in which he was held during antiquity. It is, allegedly, 91 BCE, and Cato is an orphaned four-year-old child. A family friend, Pompaedius Silo, is visiting the house, and Cato—who, despite his tender age, has apparently been challenging Silo on public policy—upsets Silo so much that he grabs the boy by his an-kles and dangles him outside a window, threatening to let him go unless Cato agrees that the land reforms proposed by Silo's party are good for Rome. Cato just stares at his captor without budging until the other gives up, pulls him back, and says, "How lucky for Italy that he is a boy; if he were a man, I don't think we could get a single vote."[4] That ought to give you a measure of the kid's character!

As usual with Plutarch, this story is meant to convey a truth about the future man and to impart a moral lesson, not neces-sarily to be biographically accurate. The relevant political back-ground here is complex. Land reform had been attempted before in the Roman Republic and had led to the gruesome deaths of Rome's most famous radicals, the Gracchi brothers, Tiberius and

Gaius. The Gracchi, representatives of the plebeians, were making very reasonable demands about the redistribution of land, wanting to take some out of the hands of a few powerful aristocrats and give it to small farmers. These demands, if met, might have forestalled or even prevented the decline of the Republic and its descent—or ascent, depending on your point of view—into empire. But the aristocrats were powerful enough to stop attempts at reform, both legally and, eventually, by bloodying the streets of the capital with the blood of the two brothers—after which they had the gall to build a new Temple of Concord to celebrate the "reunification" of the people of Rome.

The struggle initiated by the Gracchi went on for a decade and resulted in the solidifying of two political factions: the *populares* (men of the people) and the *optimates* (literally the best people, i.e., the aristocracy). Cato became a lifelong member of the *optimates*, which eventually put him on a collision course with Julius Caesar, who sought the support of the *populares*. But I'm getting ahead of the story.

Interestingly, Cato's own uncle and legal guardian, Marcus Livius Drusus, was a supporter of the popular reforms, which is presumably why he had invited Silo to his house. But the rest of the Senate opposed Drusus and managed to reverse some legislation he had been able to pass. He was soon killed in his own house by an unknown man.

Shortly thereafter, the Republic became engulfed in a civil war between two generals, Lucius Cornelius Sulla and Gaius Marius. Sulla eventually won and named himself dictator for life. The title "dictator" was conferred by the Senate on an extraordinary individual in times of extreme peril and was supposed to be relinquished after the danger had passed. It seems that Sulla forgot that detail or perhaps was convinced that Rome was in permanent danger and therefore would need him for the rest of his life. Sulla turned out to have little respect for either law or tradition, embarking on a spree of killing his political opponents and, moreover, on a systematic campaign of confiscating their properties to enrich himself and his cronies.

As an aside, Sulla was indirectly responsible, of all things, for the spread of philosophy to Rome. Since Athens had sided with the king of Pontus, Mithridates, against Rome, Sulla laid siege to the ancient Greek city, entered it, and burned it. This destruction of Athens resulted in the sudden diaspora of a large number of philosophers, including the Stoics, who relocated to various places, chiefly Alexandria, Rhodes, and, of course, Rome.

This background is crucial to understand Cato's whole life and the development of his philosophical perspective. As biographers Goodman and Soni put it, "Cato and his half brother often sat by Sulla's side [because they were aristocrats, often invited by Sulla], eyewitnesses to the arbitrary power of a man fond of making the Senate listen to his harangues and the cries of the executed at the same time."[5]

While Sulla did quash any attempt at land reform—and should therefore be counted among the ranks of the *optimates*— he did so without regard for Roman law, a fact that he fully realized, to the point that he actually introduced legislation aimed at preventing another meteoric rise such as his own from ever happening again. He apparently thought of the objective of his autocratic government as ending all future autocratic governments. Needless to say, it did not work. Quite the contrary, in fact, since Sulla's actions provided an excellent precedent for those of Julius Caesar, which in turn led directly to the establishment of the Empire under Caesar's adoptive son, Octavian.

But back to Cato. We already have a complex image of him. On the one hand, he was an aristocrat opposed to land reforms that were both just and in the long-term interest of the very thing he cared the most about, the Republic. On the other hand, he had personally observed, as a youth, just how absolutely power concentrated in a single man can corrupt, which brings me to a second episode from his early life, this one likely closer to the actual historical record. One day, while returning home with his tutor from one of Sulla's horrific sessions, Cato asked why nobody got rid of the dictator. The tutor told him that "men fear him more than they hate him." Cato promptly responded, "Give me a sword, so I might kill him and set my country free of slavery." From that day on, his tutor wisely checked whether Cato was hiding a dagger every time they left the house.

Cato launched his political career at age twenty-eight, submitting his name for the office of military tribune, a classic stepping-stone to the Senate. He distinguished himself on the campaign trail by refusing to canvass for votes with the aid of a "nomenclator." Traditionally, a nomenclator was a person in charge of reminding a candidate who the people he was asking for money were and helping him pretend that he knew them better than he actually did. This false charm was not Cato's style, however. No subterfuges or tricks. He approached potential voters on his own, and if he didn't know them, he would frankly admit it and engage them anyway. It worked. He was elected for 67 BCE and given a command in Macedonia as part of Roman operations against the old foe, Mithridates.

Cato joined a fully professional army whose soldiers were difficult to impress, particularly when they expected a city slicker who would spend a year with them just so that he could build credentials for the next move in his political career. But Cato's soldiers were in for a surprise. To begin with, he arrived at the camp on foot, not on horseback, as was customary for Roman officers. Even more surprisingly, his style of relating to his men was very unusual. Instead of punishing them when they disagreed, for instance, he always tried to reason with them.

His practice of Stoic philosophy was useful to him as a commander and, later, as a provincial administrator in Cyprus. One major reason why Cato's leadership style was effective with his troops was that he did more than just talk about Stoicism. He put the philosophy into actual practice, and his men loved and respected him for it. When he left the army, they threw their cloaks on the ground so that he would walk on them.

Cato took a furlough from the legions and spent some time in Pergamon, the ancient city in Asia Minor famous for the production of parchment and for housing one of the most complete libraries of antiquity. There lived the renowned Stoic Athenodorus, presiding over what is reported to be more than 200,000 scrolls, which included the writings of the original Greek Stoics. Several of these had not yet appeared in Rome, and Cato could now consult them at his leisure. What a deep shame that the entire library has been lost to the sands of time. Cato and Athenodorus became friends, and when the latter was threatened because he had allegedly edited some of the Stoic texts, Cato offered him protection. Athenodorus eventually sailed back to Rome with Cato and died there several years later.

Shortly after returning to his legion, Cato received a letter notifying him that his half brother, Caepio—who was serving in the same theater of operations—was seriously ill. The two brothers were very close, and when Caepio died, Cato embraced his brother's body and wept bitterly. After the funeral, Cato commissioned a massive marble bust of Caepio to be displayed publicly. This episode haunted Cato for the rest of his life. His critics cited these actions as a demonstration of the uselessness of his much-vaunted philosophy. After all, isn't death, for a Stoic, just a natural phenomenon to be accepted with equanimity, even when it strikes his loved ones? Isn't a statue a pretentious way to honor someone's memory? Such criticism, however, is rather uncharitable, as Cato most certainly did live, and die, largely in accordance with his Stoic philosophy. He wasn't faking it; he was the genuine article.

Let's jump forward to 63 BCE, when Senator Lucius Sergius Catilina organized a conspiracy to overthrow his colleagues and implement (again!) radical land reforms that would have redistributed much of the wealth in the Republic, taking it away from the few aristocrats who held it and giving it to, among others, a number of disgruntled veterans of recent wars. It was yet another iteration of the long-established opposition between the *populares* and the *optimates*.

That said, we need not attribute noble sentiments to Catilina, who was a bankrupt aristocrat in search of redemption and a new shot at public life. By this time in his career, Catilina—whose attempts to be elected consul had been thwarted by (possibly unfounded) charges of corruption—had had enough of laws and regulations and had concluded that only violent means would achieve his objectives.

Enter Cicero, the great orator, philosopher, and statesman. He was a rising political star in Rome who came from a non-aristocratic background and was better able than anyone else to perceive what Catilina was up to. Cicero mounted a series of preemptive strikes against Catilina, including running for the office of consul that year, in order to forestall the impending disaster. The aristocracy supported Cicero, not because they particularly liked him, as he was, in effect, an outsider, but because they were desperate to avoid the Catiline revolution.

In the same year, Cato ran for the post of tribune of the plebeians, which was rather odd given his allegiance to the *optimates*. It was, however, legal, as Cato's family technically did not belong to the Roman aristocracy. Cato and Cicero at first joined forces against what they saw as a mortal threat to the very existence of the Republic. Cicero had been warning his fellow citizens about Catilina for a while, but his warnings had largely been unheeded. In fact, the other senators began to suspect that the threat was being invented, or at least exaggerated, by Cicero himself to further his career. However, one of Cicero's allies, the military commander and stupendously rich Marcus Licinius Crassus, was able to provide hard evidence of the Catiline conspiracy in the form of a letter describing detailed plans to murder a number of senators opposed to the reforms.

Cato was present at the emergency meeting of the Senate called by Cicero, at the end of which the latter was given extraordinary powers to swiftly end the conspiracy. When, shortly thereafter, Cicero publicly confronted Catilina, the latter responded by illegally declaring himself consul and then promptly fleeing the city to join his army, camped not far away.

Here is where things get complicated as well as interesting because they help us draw a sharp distinction between the two friends, soon to be rivals, Cicero and Cato. During the previous summer, the consular election had been won by Lucius Lucinius Murena, a former legionary commander, and Decimus Junius Silanus. Both had achieved their goal by way of (not at all uncommon) massive bribes. Cicero had pushed a new law—with the important and very vocal support of Cato—that raised the penalty for bribery to ten years of exile. Murena, who was scheduled to take over as consul in a few months, was swiftly brought up on charges of corruption. Cicero, somewhat unexpectedly, offered to defend Murena, while Cato was set to deliver the closing argument against him, following which Cicero would be allowed time for a rebuttal before the outcome of the trial would be decided.

Now, why on earth did Cicero agree to defend a man who was patently guilty, especially given that Cicero himself had worked hard to pass the anticorruption law? The contrast in behavior between Cato and Cicero illuminates the distinction between a politician whose actions are strictly informed by his philosophy and one whose actions are guided largely by (principled) pragmatism. Cicero's main concern was the threat posed by Catilina, and he gave that the utmost priority. In order to face that threat, he needed to rely on the support of the two new consuls, corrupt as they might have been. That was why he wanted Murena acquitted. By contrast, Cato acted on the basis of his Stoic idealism, which told him that it was his duty to prosecute a corrupt politician.

The contrast between Cicero and Cato should give us plenty of food for thought at many levels. They were both philosophically minded, though one was primarily a lawyer, the other a soldier and politician. They espoused different philosophies— skeptical Platonism in Cicero's case and Stoicism in Cato's, though Cicero was also very sympathetic to Stoicism. And they both indubitably cared for the future of the Roman Republic, though in different ways and perhaps with different priorities.

As a result, they found themselves locked in a strange relationship of both friendship and rivalry throughout the best part of their lives. On the one hand, Cicero displayed political savvy and an ability to compromise in order to achieve his objectives, though his readiness to adjust to the situation on the ground at times bordered on hypocrisy or opportunism. On the other hand, Cato was the light of virtue and integrity that inspired his followers and was much admired by Cicero. But that same uncompromising virtue led to Cato's failure to build the sort of political coalition that might have turned the fortunes of the Republic and avoided its disintegration into empire.

During the trial, Cato took the stage to present his case against Murena, and Cicero delivered the rebuttal. Cicero mercilessly mocked his friend both for his high moral stand and for the source from which that stand derived, his Stoic philosophy. Cato was no match for Cicero's rhetoric, and Murena was duly acquitted. But Cato took the defeat in stride. His only comment after the proceedings were over was "What a witty consul we have!"

Cato's magnanimity was in full view shortly thereafter, when he didn't have to think twice to agree to defend Cicero from the accusation of attempting to abuse his emergency powers during the Catiline conspiracy. That defense was pitted against the accusations of a young, ambitious politician named Gaius Julius Caesar. In the end, the conspirators were executed, as recommended by Cicero, and Cato marched at the head of a crowd shouting, "Cicero, father of the Fatherland!"

Think about this for a moment. Despite the recent humiliation handed to him by Cicero, Cato helped bring the orator to the highest point of his political life, not because it was expedient but because—in Cato's mind—it was the right thing to do. The defeated Caesar, however, learned his lesson well, and prepared for the next confrontation by allying himself even more forcefully with the *populares*, laying the ground for his ascent to the dictatorship, which eventually caused the final unraveling of the Republic and the beginning of the Empire.

Caesar's course of action led to a civil war and eventually to Cato's last stand against the dictator, which took place in the northern African city of Utica (hence his alternate name, Cato Uticensis) in 47 BCE. How did they get there? Three years earlier, Caesar, after a very successful military campaign in Gaul, had been ordered to disband his army and return to Rome to stand trial for corruption, instigated by Cato's political faction, the *optimates*. Following a stalemate and failed negotiations, Caesar crossed the River Rubicon with a single legion—an act that amounted to treason against the Republic—allegedly uttering the famous words "*Alea iacta est*" (The die is cast).

General Pompey, who had issued the order to Caesar to desist and surrender himself, fled Rome, together with many senators, including Cato. Cato was unhappy about this, having become a highly reluctant ally of Pompey, whom he judged merely to be the lesser of two evils when compared to Caesar. Caesar pursued Pompey, Cato, and the other senators in the east, in Illyria, but in 48 BCE, the Caesarean forces were almost annihilated at the battle of Dyrrhachium. On that occasion, Pompey made the fatal strategic mistake of not pursuing his opponent's fleeing legions and paid a hefty price at their next engagement, later that same year at Pharsalus, where he was soundly defeated. This time, Pompey's men were on the run. Pompey turned to King Ptolemy XII of Egypt for asylum but was betrayed and slain as soon as he stepped off his boat. Caesar, horrified by this outcome, deposed Ptolemy in favor of his sister, Cleopatra VII, who famously became his lover.

Meanwhile, the remaining republican forces regrouped in northern Africa, heading for the provincial capital of Utica with Cato at their head. An army of about ten thousand men marched for five hundred miles in the desert. It took them about thirty days to get to Utica, and the poet Lucan tells us in verse how Cato bore himself during that ordeal:[6]

> Bearing his javelin, as one of them
> Before the troops he marched: no panting slave
> With bending neck, no litter bore his form.
> He bade them not, but showed them how to toil.
> Spare in his sleep, the last to sip the spring
> When at some rivulet to quench their thirst
> The eager ranks pressed onward, he alone
> Until the humblest follower might drink
> Stood motionless.

But when Cato's army arrived in Utica, they found their allies in complete disarray. Rather than organizing a resistance that, with luck, could hold off Caesar for years, they squabbled about who had the highest rank and should command the effort. The contenders were Publius Attius Varus, who had been a commander in the region; Metellus Scipio, an ex-consul; and Juba, the king of Numidia. Cato's arrival immediately changed the situation, given that he was now the most famous and prestigious member of the resistance. Biographers Goodman and Soni describe the scene: "Without a word, Cato simply picked up his chair, walked around the king and the ex-consul, and placed his chair on the other side—which gave Metellus Scipio pride of place in the center."[7]

Cato decided to support Scipio because the latter was the highest-ranking officer, and Cato saw himself as fighting to uphold the law that he had far too many times seen trampled by ambitious men, from Sulla in his youth to Caesar now. Here, however, is another case where it is surely legitimate to criticize

Cato. Despite the fact that Scipio was indeed the highest rank-
ing of the group, he was manifestly less competent than Cato
himself, and Cato's choice arguably was the main cause of the
disaster that eventually followed. Was Cato risking too much in
the name of the purity of his ideals? Plutarch comments on the
episode, "He refused to break the laws in whose support they
were waging war [against] one who broke them."[8]

Cato may have passed on the opportunity to take complete
charge of the situation, but he nonetheless played an important
role in the last days of the republican resistance against Caesar.
At one point, for instance, Scipio and Juba became suspicious
of the inhabitants of Utica, thinking that they wanted to betray
them and open the city's doors to Caesar's army. As a preemptive measure, the two wanted to raze the city and kill its people.
Cato was the voice of opposition and carried the day, thus sparing the lives of many.

The first engagement between Scipio's republican forces and
Caesar ended in almost complete defeat for the dictator, whose
army suffered great losses and was saved at the last minute from
encirclement and utter destruction. Scipio, energized by the victory, wanted to again engage Caesar in open battle, but Cato—
who had seen and studied his opponent for years—counseled
against it. Scipio wrote to Cato that he was a coward and on
April 6, 46 BCE, gave battle to Caesar anyway. It was a disaster,
and the republican forces were vanquished.

In the wake of the defeat, the situation in Utica looked grim.
Three hundred resident Roman merchants and moneylenders
swore to defend the city and Cato with their lives. But eventually they took back their pledge, committing only to fight for
Cato's own life in the unlikely case that Caesar would not con-
cede clemency. They excused their less-than-principled change

of heart with a phrase that had become common in Rome: "We are not Catos."

Cato, however, wasn't done being Cato just yet. In the chaotic aftermath of the defeat, the republican cavalry left in Utica began to loot the city, pillaging and killing the locals. Cato intervened again on behalf of the populace, and since he was unable to persuade the soldiers by way of words, he simply bribed them with his own money to go away. Despite fatigue and stress, Cato remained true to his Stoic ideals, turning his priorities toward enabling the citizens of Utica to flee before the arrival of Caesar's forces. He even used his own resources to pay for those too poor to afford the passage.

In the end, he was left with his family and two philosopher friends, Apollonides the Stoic and Demetrius the Aristotelian. Now Cato had to decide what to do with himself, as it was clear that Caesar would pardon him, not just out of respect but also to establish his dictatorship on a higher moral ground than that offered by the arbitrary slaughterhouse that Rome had seen under Sulla.

After a last dinner and philosophical conversation with Apollonides and Demetrius, Cato retired to his room to read Plato's *Phaedo*. He already had his dagger, brought to him by his attendant earlier that evening. His family had guessed what his intentions were, but Cato had vociferously demanded his weapon.

The *Phaedo* recounts the last hours of Socrates's life, which were spent in philosophical conversation with his friends. Once he finished his reading, Cato picked up his dagger and attempted to stab himself to death. Painfully, the attempt failed due to a hand injury incurred in battle. Plutarch supplies details on what happened next:

Cato did not immediately die of the wound; but struggling, fell off the bed, and throwing down a little mathematical table that stood by, made such a noise that the servants, hearing it, cried out. And immediately his son and all his friends came into the chamber, where, seeing him lie weltering in his own blood, great part of his bowels out of his body, but himself still alive and able to look at them, they all stood in horror. The physician went to him, and would have put in his bowels, which were not pierced, and sewed up the wound; but Cato, recovering himself, and understanding the intention, thrust away the physician, plucked out his own bowels, and tearing open the wound, immediately expired.[9]

How's that for an example of philosophy informing the actions of a statesman? According to Plutarch, upon hearing the news, Caesar remarked, "Cato, I grudge you your death, as you would have grudged me the preservation of your life."[10]

Despite his questionable—by modern standards—political allegiance to the *optimates* and his ultimate failure to save the Republic, Cato's legacy has endured, which makes him a good case study for our purposes. Even shortly after his death, Octavian Augustus—Julius Caesar's nephew and the first Roman emperor—actually embraced (in theory, at least) both republican values and Cato's memory, probably because Octavian was a savvier politician than Caesar himself. Once, when visiting Cato's house, he interrupted a sycophant who was criticizing the Stoic senator, replying, "To seek to keep the established constitution unchanged is a sign of a good citizen and a good man."[11] Cato also appears in Virgil's *Aeneid*, the epic poem commissioned by Augustus to provide a strong mythological root for the founding of Rome and, indirectly, for the empire he created.

I mentioned that the Stoic philosopher Seneca considered Cato one of his role models. Lucan, who was Seneca's nephew, wrote the poem *Pharsalia* (named after the battle where Caesar defeated Pompey), which was originally intended to be in praise of Nero but ended up a scathing criticism of the regime. He too contributed to the myth of Cato by writing, "The victorious cause was dear to the gods; the lost cause, to Cato."[12]

Eventually the Christians came on the scene and had to reckon with Cato as well. Suicide was not admissible for the new religion, and Cato was most famous (and most admired) precisely for the way he had walked through what the Stoic philosopher Epictetus termed "the open door." The Christian approach was to chide Cato for basically showing off, especially in death. From their perspective, he was guilty of the sin of pride. And yet, even Christian authors couldn't avoid admiring Cato. Tertullian, for instance, criticized the Romans for failing to deify the Stoic figure! Augustine was both a harsh critic and a great admirer of Cato and considered him almost a pre-Christian sage in terms of virtue.

Centuries later, at the dawn of humanism, Dante gave Cato a prime role in his *Divine Comedy*, having the Stoic stand guard at the entrance of the Mountain of Purgatory because, as the poet put it, "What man on earth was more worthy to signify God than Cato? Surely none."[13] Dante spared Cato from Hell because, although he was a pagan and died by his own hand, he died for the cause of freedom. That set the stage for a new phase of Cato's legacy: as a revolutionary and a personification of secular virtue.

During the late seventeenth century, Joseph Addison wrote a play titled *Cato: A Tragedy*. It became influential in both the old and the new world. It was rich in aphorisms, which came to be regularly deployed by the likes of Benjamin Franklin and

John Adams, among others. George Washington used quotations from the play to inspire his revolutionary troops at Valley Forge. Incidentally, we know Washington began to read Seneca at age seventeen, and biographer Ron Chernow writes, "As his life progressed, Washington would adhere to the Stoic creed of governing one's passions under the most adverse circumstances and facing the prospect of death with serenity."[14]

The reception of Addison's *Cato* also demonstrates the attraction that ancient wisdom or philosophy has for ruling factions and statesmen regardless of their political affinities. When the play was staged in England, both Tories and Whigs fell in love with it, vying to identify their party and their values with the main character. Alexander Pope writes that "Cato was not so much the wonder of Rome itself in his days as he is of Britain in ours,"[15] while Voltaire calls Cato "the greatest character that was brought upon any stage."[16] When Addison's play reached America, its success was unmatched until Arthur Miller's *Death of a Salesman*.

Cato's fame continued to develop in unexpected ways. As biographers Goodman and Soni point out, in 1720, a series of anonymous letters began to appear in the *London Journal*, signed only "Cato." An example reads, "Thus it is that liberty is almost everywhere lost: Her foes are artful, united and diligent: Her defenders are few, disunited, and inactive.... This passion for liberty in men, and their possession of it, is of that efficacy and importance, that it seems the parent of all the virtues."[17] The collected 144 letters by "Cato" became a best seller, popularizing ideas about natural rights and limited government. It is in reference to those letters that the libertarian think tank the Cato Institute is named.

And so we arrive at our own times. Cato the Younger remains, more than two thousand years after his death, a looming figure in Western history. Our modern minds question the myth, of course, but the real man compels us because—not in spite—of his failings. Assuming we don't want another Caesar to take charge, the more complicated question for us becomes the following: Do we want our politicians to be more inspired by Cato or by Cicero?

CASE STUDY TWO: MARCUS AURELIUS

Marcus Aurelius Antoninus Augustus was one of the so-called five good Roman emperors who presided over the period of the most expansion, splendor, and relative peace that the Roman Empire ever enjoyed (the other four, preceding Marcus, were Nerva, Trajan, Hadrian, and Antoninus Pius—the Nerva-Antonine dynasty). He was one of the few philosopher-kings on record and hence an excellent case study for our preoccupation with the relationship between philosophy, character, and statesmanship. Marcus had a happy youth but a tormented reign. He was born in Rome in 121 CE to a wealthy family that owned a number of brick factories and had significant political influence. He was noticed and protected by the emperor Hadrian, who instructed his chosen successor, Antoninus Pius, to adopt Marcus as well as Lucius Verus and to groom them both for the throne. Marcus did become emperor in 161 CE, after the death of Antoninus, and he immediately appointed the far less capable Lucius as co-emperor (Lucius died in 169 CE, probably of the plague, leaving Marcus sole emperor).

Marcus had married Faustina, daughter of Antoninus, in 145 CE, and the two eventually had thirteen children, of whom only five daughters and one son survived into adulthood. Unfortunately for the Roman people, that son was the infamous

Commodus, to whom I shall return later. Trouble began the very same year that Marcus and Lucius Verus ascended to the throne, when the Parthians—the longtime rivals of the Romans in the east—invaded a number of Roman provinces. It took several years and the capable leadership of Generals Statius Priscus and Avidius Cassius to push back the Parthians. In 166 CE, as soon as the ceremonies for the victory had been held, the Marcomanni and the Quadi threatened the northern frontier with what today is Germany. Consequently Marcus had to carry out military campaigns in the Danube region from 169 to 175 CE, and it was during this time that he likely wrote his famous *Meditations*, an example of the personal philosophical diary that provides us with unique insight into the mind of a Roman emperor who was also a practicing Stoic.

Marcus's philosophy guided him through still more challenges. As soon as he had quelled the Marcomanni and Quadi situation, Avidius Cassius rebelled and declared himself emperor and then was subdued by Martius Verus, the loyal governor of Cappadocia (modern Turkey). Marcus next embarked on an extended trip east with his wife, Faustina. The empress, however, died en route. Despite her reputation as an adulteress, Marcus remembers Faustina tenderly in the *Meditations*.

During his reign as emperor, Marcus faced not just war and rebellion but also a number of other calamities, including major flooding of the Tiber River (161 CE), a plague (166 CE) that took millions of lives throughout the empire, and a gigantic earthquake in Smyrna (Turkey, 178 CE). After his return to Rome, he had to leave again to engage in another northern campaign, and he died, most likely at Vienna, in 180 CE. As commentator Cassius Dio aptly puts it, "He didn't have the luck which he deserved ... but was confronted, throughout his reign, by a multitude of disasters. That is why I admire him more than any other, for it was amidst these extraordinary and unparalleled difficulties that he was able to survive, and to save the Empire."[18]

Marcus was a philosopher, but not, of course, in the modern sense of an academic profession. As I mentioned above, in antiquity, a philosopher could be a teacher but also could be anyone who actually practiced a chosen philosophy of life. There are two documents that testify to Marcus's interest in philosophy and his adoption of Stoicism in particular: his correspondence with his teacher of rhetoric, Marcus Cornelius Fronto, and, of course, the *Meditations*. It appears that his conversion to Stoicism was due to the work of Junius Rusticus, a mentor who introduced Marcus to the work of the influential Stoic teacher Epictetus, for which introduction Marcus thanked Rusticus in the first book of the *Meditations*.[19] But Marcus's interest in philosophy as a way of life dated back to when he was twelve years old. Another teacher, Diognetus, is credited in the *Meditations* for instilling in Marcus "the desire to sleep on a cot and a simple animal-skin, and for things of this sort which belong to the Hellenic way of life."[20]

Although Marcus had a number of mentors, Rusticus was his favorite teacher, according to the *Historia Augusta*, and Marcus consulted him on both private and public business. Rusticus was both Marcus's friend and his spiritual guide, as we would say today. Interestingly, a reference to Rusticus reveals something about Marcus's character. In his *Meditations*,[21] Marcus thanks Rusticus for teaching him not to become angry with people who irritate him, which apparently was a weakness that Marcus had identified in himself. This is what good philosophy helps us with: becoming conscious of our own faults and constantly practicing to gradually reduce them.

We learn some more about Marcus's character and philosophy from reading his youthful correspondence with his teacher of rhetoric, Fronto. At one point, Marcus wrote to Fronto that he was absorbed by his study of Aristo, who—to Fronto's horror—had reminded him that those who conduct advanced studies of dialectics are like people eating crayfish: They struggle with a lot of shell for very little nourishment. The warning also aligns with the Stoic attitude toward devoting oneself to theoretical matters. That sort of study is okay to a point, so long as the theory is actually useful in practice to help us live a good life. But beyond that level, we engage in studying for erudition's sake, something the Stoics thought would lead to damaging attitudes, such as argumentation that uses logic chopping or rhetorical flourishing.

Marcus also went to formal school, attending the lessons of Apollonius of Chalcedon and Sextus of Chaeronea. Apollonius insisted that Marcus had to come to him, not the other way around, refusing to tutor the youth at the imperial palace. This prompted a rare sarcastic response by Marcus's adoptive father, the emperor Antoninus Pius, who commented that he had brought Apollonius from far away at great expense to teach Marcus, but it had been easier to persuade the philosopher to leave his native Chalcedon (modern western Turkey) to come to Rome than it now was to persuade him to leave his quarters in the capital to come to the palace.

Providing a good example for all of us, Marcus valued philosophical study even when he was older, when he attended Sextus's school. He was criticized for this and responded, "Learning is a good thing, even for one who is growing old. From Sextus the philosopher I shall learn what I do not know yet."[22]

When Marcus became emperor on March 7, 161 CE, Fronto the rhetorician was not happy about his intention to govern in a philosophical manner. Rather sarcastically, he wrote to Marcus, "Even should you attain the wisdom of Cleanthes or of Zeno [the second and first heads of the Stoa, respectively], you shall still be obliged, like it or not, to wear the purple pallium, and not that of the philosophers, made of coarse wool."[23] That is, you may be a philosopher, but as an emperor, you'll still need to deploy the rhetorical skills I taught you in order to govern effectively. Nevertheless, Marcus did his best to govern as a philosopher, surrounding himself with philosophers as advisers. Apparently the people of Rome were well aware of this fact and arguably benefited from it. Indeed, Galen—the most famous doctor of antiquity, who was Marcus's personal physician—testifies to an intense philosophical activity during Marcus's reign within the circles of the Roman aristocracy.

The major source for understanding Marcus as a person is the *Meditations*. The book begins with a long exercise in gratitude, where the emperor thanks all the people who influenced him for the better, detailing what he learned from each one. In a sense, the *Meditations* are Marcus's "confessions," analogous to some extent to the famous book by the same title written by Augustine of Hippo. The first chapters in particular can be read as a personal spiritual itinerary from childhood to the discovery of philosophy, and especially its practice: "To have known Apollonius, Rusticus, Maximus. To have had clear and frequent representations of the 'life according to nature,' so that, insofar as it depends on the gods and on the communications, assistance, and inspirations which come from above, nothing now prevents me from living 'according to nature'; but I am far from that point by my own fault, because I pay no attention to the reminders, or rather to the teachings, which come from the gods."[24]

"Living according to nature," for the Stoics, meant living while keeping in mind the distinctive characteristics of the human animal: our ability to reason and our prosociality. The humility that is evident in this passage is seen elsewhere in the *Meditations*, for instance, when Marcus freely admits that people have a point when they remark on the limits of his intelligence: "They can hardly admire your quickness of mind. So be it! But there are many other things about which you cannot say 'I am not gifted.' Show us, then, all these things that depend entirely on you: being without duplicity, being serious,... being free."[25]

The obvious issue that is often raised about Marcus's character is whether he was sincere or affected. The emperor Hadrian, who picked Marcus for the line of succession after Antoninus Pius, nicknamed Marcus Verissimus, that is, the very sincere. And historian Cassius Dio, who lived during the reign of Commodus, Marcus's infamous son, writes, "[Marcus Aurelius] obviously did nothing out of affectation, but everything out of virtue.... To such an extent was he truly a good man, and there was nothing affected about him."[26]

How exactly did Marcus balance his duties as emperor and his vocation as a philosopher? This, of course, is a crucial question because it speaks directly to our concerns here. Marcus often reminds himself that he is, in a sense, a prisoner of the halls of power and that he will always be surrounded by people who will attempt to take advantage of his favor. He compares court life to a stepmother, while his true mother is philosophy. A highly pertinent point made by Pierre Hadot concerns the inevitable conflicts between Marcus's duties as an emperor and as a practicing Stoic: "These two duties are hard to reconcile: on the one hand, our duty [as Stoics] to love other human beings, with whom we form one single body, tree, or city [various metaphors used by Marcus]; on the other, our duty not to let ourselves be cajoled into adopting their false values and maxims of life."[27]

A related question concerns the relationship between Stoicism and political programs. How did Marcus—as emperor—approach the issue? One clue is found in his own explicit list of political role models, which included Paetus Thrasea, Helvidius Priscus, Cato the Younger, Marcus Junius Brutus, and Dio of Syracuse. The first two were members of the so-called Stoic opposition against the tyranny of Vespasian. Cato we encountered above. Brutus was the chief conspirator against Caesar. And Dio deposed the infamous tyrant of Syracuse, Dionysius II, the fellow who almost got Plato killed, as we saw in the last chapter. The common factor among all of these men is that they put their lives on the line to fight against tyranny and for what they regarded as liberty (albeit usually limited to the male dominant class). It is highly indicative that Marcus mentions them with admiration.[28] Accordingly, Marcus articulates his own ideal for how to run the Roman Empire: "A State in which the laws are equal for all, administered on the basis of equality and freedom of speech, and of a monarchy that respects the freedom of its subjects above all else."[29]

This is absolutely remarkable, especially given the time. Yes, Marcus is still a monarch, but he wants to reign by collaborating with the Senate and while respecting equality and freedom of speech, ideals not yet fully realized even in modern democracies. But how much progress did Marcus actually make? Let's briefly examine three controversial issues facing the famous philosopher-king: the institution of slavery, the treatment of the rising sect of Christianity, and his unfortunate decision to nominate his son, Commodus, as heir to the throne.

Let's begin with the issue of slavery. The Stoic position on this was clear and highly unusual for the time: slavery, as Zeno of Citium—the founder of the Stoic sect—put it in his *Republic*, is evil. This unequivocal condemnation stems from two Stoic principles: natural law and cosmopolitanism. The Stoics believed that we should "live according to nature," meaning that we should understand the nature of the human animal and act in order to fulfill its potential. There are no natural slaves, so slavery is against nature. In terms of cosmopolitanism, this is the doctrine that all human beings are brothers and sisters, regardless of gender, ethnicity, or any other characteristic, because we all share in the fundamental attributes of humanity: our capacity for reason and our high degree of sociality. If we are all equal and if the virtue of justice mandates that we treat others with dignity, respect, and fairness, it again follows that slavery is out of the question.

Some Stoic authors did not go so far as to question the institution of slavery but nevertheless forcefully insisted that slaves are human beings like anyone else and ought to be treated accordingly. Here, for instance, is Seneca: "Kindly remember that he whom you call your slave sprang from the same stock, is smiled upon by the same skies, and on equal terms with yourself breathes, lives, and dies."[30]

Others agreed with Zeno in his criticism of the institution. One of them was Dio Chrysostom, who is mentioned by Marcus in the *Meditations*. In his discourse *On Slavery and Freedom*, Dio argues that all slaves ultimately either are themselves captured or are descended from someone who was captured, either in war or by brigands: "If, then, this original mode of acquiring slaves, from which all other modes derive their existence, be destitute of justice, none of them can consequently be deemed just; nor can a single individual either be a slave in reality, or be truly and substantially discriminated by such an appellation."[31]

The Stoic philosophy of Epictetus—a former slave—had a deep influence on Marcus. Here Epictetus describes slavery as an abhorrent institution: "What you avoid suffering yourself, seek not to impose on others. You avoid slavery, for instance; take care not to enslave. For if you can bear to exact slavery from others, you appear to have been yourself a slave. For vice has nothing in common with virtue, nor freedom with slavery."[32]

All of this is in sharp contrast with the then more commonly accepted Aristotelian position, which regarded some people as natural slaves who ought to be treated accordingly: "Those who are as different [from other men] as the soul from the body or man from beast—and they are in this state if their work is the use of the body, and if this is the best that can come from them—are slaves by nature. For them it is better to be ruled in accordance with this sort of rule, if such is the case for the other things mentioned."[33]

Nevertheless, did Marcus, in his capacity as emperor, abolish slavery? No. Nor could he have done so even if he wanted to. As author Donald Robertson reminds us, Roman society (as well as most other societies in the world at that time) fundamentally depended on slavery, and an emperor who attempted to get rid of it would have very shortly met his end. However, we know from the historical record that Marcus was concerned about the plague of slaves and that he passed several pieces of legislation to lessen their burden.

The *Historia Augusta* tells us, for instance, that Marcus resettled the defeated German tribes inside the empire instead of doing what most of his predecessors had done: execute or enslave them. More to the point, Anthony Birley and Paul Barron Watson, in their respective biographies of Marcus Aurelius, detail a considerable number of legislative acts and legal precedents promulgated or established by the emperor to ease the life of slaves. He made slave manumission, that is, the ability of owners to free their slaves, much easier to accomplish as well as more resilient to legal challenges. He confirmed a law, first enacted by his predecessor, Antoninus Pius, that an owner would stand trial when accused of murdering a slave. Watson writes, "How to augment the relatively small free population and how to alleviate the distress of the slaves and freedmen, were problems which Marcus kept continually before him.... To convince the Roman people that a person taken in war is not the property of the captor was more than any one emperor could accomplish. Marcus Aurelius did a noble work in promulgating this doctrine; but its final adoption could only be effected by the reasoning of ages."[34]

One example of how Marcus attempted to further his progressive doctrine is a law he passed that required owners to sue their slaves in court if they thought a slave had done them wrong. Before the change went into effect, the owner had the right to put the slave to death for any reason that he pleased. With the same law, Marcus also sought to do away with the *quaestio*, the practice by which a slave suspected of a crime could be tortured by the owner until he or she confessed. By a different decree, Marcus then made it illegal to sell slaves in order to pit them against wild beasts in the arena, a "game" that could result in only one gruesome outcome.

None of this amounts to the abolition of slavery, or anywhere near it. But as the modern historian of philosophy Bertrand Russell aptly puts it, "[The Stoics'] was an ideal which could not be consistently realized in the Roman Empire, but it influenced legislation, particularly in improving the status of women and slaves. Christianity took over this part of Stoic teaching along with much of the rest. And when at last, in the seventeenth century, the opportunity came to combat despotism effectually, the Stoic doctrines of natural law and natural equality, in their Christian dress, acquired a practical force which, in antiquity, not even an emperor could give to them."[35]

Sadly it was perhaps too early in the moral development of human societies to expect a Roman emperor such as Marcus (or an Egyptian pharaoh, or pretty much any other ancient ruler) to fully challenge the institution of slavery. Still, another issue has long been damaging to Marcus's reputation: his alleged persecution of the Christians. However, translator and commentator C. R. Haines (Delphi Classics) observes that those who think Marcus persecuted the Christians base this conclusion on doubtful circumstantial evidence, which in fact goes directly against the testimony of Christian writers of the time regarding Marcus's character: "His *filanthropia* [love of humanity] is mentioned by Galen, Dio, Philostratus, Athenagoras (twice), Melito, and Aristides (eleven times); and his *humanitas* [kindness] by the eminent jurist Callistratus."[36] Marcus himself writes in the eighth book of the *Meditations* (which, remember, was not meant for publication, so he wasn't boasting), "Never have I willingly injured another,"[37] which agrees with his well-documented passion for justice and observance of the law.

It is true that during Marcus's reign, some Christians suffered for their religion at the hands of local governors, but the governors operated with a significant degree of freedom from the central power of the emperor. Even so, we have no undisputed records of any single martyrdom from that period. More to the point, there certainly was no systematic and widespread persecution of Christians by Marcus. Christians were present and well known in Rome at the time; they had a publicly recognized bishop, and Haines reminds us that some of them were part of the emperor's own household, while others (e.g., Apollonius) were members of the Senate.

The major damning piece of evidence concerning Marcus's treatment of followers of the new religion comes from the Christian historian Eusebius and refers to an alleged massacre that took place in Lyon in Gaul in 177 CE. Donald Robertson has carried out an in-depth analysis of this source and found it wanting. One problem is that Eusebius wrote his commentary about 120 years after the alleged events, and he was known to fabricate stories in the service of his faith. Eusebius actually writes that "it will be necessary sometimes to use falsehood as a remedy for the benefit of those who require such a mode of treatment."[38] Robertson mentions that the historian Jacob Burckhardt called Eusebius the first thoroughly dishonest historian of antiquity.

Moreover, no other author—Christian or pagan—mentions the events in Lyon, while Irenaeus, who was bishop of Lyon and wrote a massive attack on pagans, *Against Heresies*, in 180, three years after the massacre allegedly happened, does not comment at all on the matter. Eusebius himself lays the blame on the mob and administrators of the city of Lyon, not on the central authority of Rome. And let me add that the Christian writer Tertullian, who was in fact a contemporary of Marcus, refers to him as a protector of Christians.

A major piece of evidence that speaks in Marcus's favor in this matter comes from a letter the emperor himself wrote to the cities of the province of Asia in 161 CE, just after his accession to the throne. In the letter, Marcus expressly forbids attacks against Christians:

> You harass these men [the Christians], and harden them in their conviction, to which they hold fast, by accusing them of being atheists. For indeed they would rather be thought to be accused and die for their own God than live. Consequently they even come off victorious, giving up their lives rather than comply with your demands.... And on behalf of such persons many Governors also of provinces have before now both written to our deified father [Antoninus Pius], whose answer in fact was not to molest such persons unless they were shown to be making some attempt in respect to the Roman Government, and to me also many have given information about such men, to whom indeed I also replied in accordance with my father's view. And if any one persist in bringing any such person into trouble for being what he is, let him, against whom the charge is brought, be acquitted even if the charge be made out, but let him who brings the charge be called to account.[39]

The latter part is especially clear: Do not persecute Christians for being Christians, and instead hold accountable those who denounce them only for their faith rather than because of demonstrable harm to the interests of Rome.

It is, however, true that the lifelong student of philosophy did not admire Christian reasoning. We can observe this in a number of relevant passages of Marcus's *Meditations* (1.6, 3.6, 7.68, 8.48.51, and 9.3). *Meditations* 9.3 in particular is interesting because of the contrast between the Christian and the Roman approach, as perceived by Marcus: "What a soul is that which is ready to be released from the body at any requisite moment, and be quenched or dissipated or hold together! But the readiness must spring from a man's inner judgment, and not be the result of mere opposition [as is the case with the Christians]. It must be associated with deliberation and dignity and, if others too are to be convinced, with nothing like stage-heroics."[40]

Here the emperor is condemning an eagerness to meet death without real justification and without due dignity, as he thought the Christians were doing. From his perspective, Christians were misguided enthusiasts who actively courted martyrdom. Despite this negative view of Christianity, however, Marcus understood that people should be free to worship their own gods and that doing so is no ground for any kind of violent action on the part of the state.

Finally, let us consider the issue of Commodus. People are often puzzled by the fact that a thoughtful emperor and Stoic philosopher such as Marcus would appoint his son Commodus to succeed him, as Commodus turned out to be a deranged tyrant who would end up being assassinated in 192 CE after having been in charge for the surprisingly long time, given the circumstances, of twelve years.

Donald Robertson, author of *How to Think Like a Roman Emperor*, has examined the complex situation in detail. He concludes that Marcus initially implemented a different succession plan, but in the end, external events forced him to appoint his son. To begin with, the default course of action for an emperor was to choose his eldest son as successor, not just because there was a natural tendency to favor one's own blood but for a couple of very practical reasons. First, because of the way the financial structure of the empire was set up, *not* to choose one's son would have meant, for all effective purposes, disinheriting him. Second, choosing someone on a meritocratic basis would have virtually guaranteed a struggle for the succession and likely a civil war. As Marcus Aurelius's biographer Frank McLynn puts it, "There were prudential reasons [to appoint one's son]. Meritocracy was all very well, but a meritocratic appointment to the purple would risk almost certain rebellion from the excluded kin of the late emperor. To appoint an emperor on mere talent and ability, then, was to hand him a poisoned chalice. When an emperor finally did exclude his own son (in 306), the result was eighteen years of civil war."[41]

True, there were exceptions. The very first emperor, Octavian Augustus, had been adopted by Julius Caesar. But Caesar was without an heir of his own. The same happened to be true for four of the five "good emperors," of whom Marcus was the last. Recall that Marcus himself had been adopted by Antoninus Pius at the suggestion of Hadrian, so Marcus had been designated, and groomed, to be emperor for a long time.

Marcus was initially a co-emperor with his adoptive brother, Lucius Verus. The expectation was actually that Lucius would succeed Marcus, as he was younger and healthier. Marcus and Lucius together appointed Commodus "caesar" (the rank below "augustus," the imperial title) when the latter was only five years old. It was a bit early to assess his character and suitability, but Commodus would eventually have become junior co-emperor with Lucius, which would have given him time to be groomed for the position. In fact, Marcus and Lucius also appointed another of Marcus's sons, Marcus Annius Verus, as caesar, again creating redundancy in the line of succession.

However, Lucius Verus died of the plague in 169 CE, and Marcus Verus died during an operation for a tumor, leaving Commodus as the only chosen caesar. We must also note that these appointments in preparation for a succession were made under pressure from the Senate when the co-emperors were about to embark on a long and perilous defensive war against the Marcomanni on the northern frontier. There was a real chance that one or both of them would not return, and plans had to be put in motion to avoid civil strife. The possibility of a civil war was very real, and we have seen that Marcus Aurelius did face a rebellion, in 175 CE, from one of his brilliant lieutenants, the ruthless Avidius Cassius.

Marcus was also unusual in making meritocratic promotions that ignored the custom of reserving the highest ranks in the military and empire for aristocrats. One pertinent case was Tiberius Claudius Pompeianus, a Syrian man of modest background who, however, fought with valor during the Parthian War. He was made the highest general on the northern border by Marcus, who also gave him his daughter Lucilla in matrimony. This made Pompeianus a member of the imperial family since Lucilla was the widow of Lucius Verus and was therefore distinguished by the title "augusta," empress. We do not know this for certain, but there was a rumor that Marcus went so far as to ask Pompeianus to become caesar to rule in the interim before Commodus was ready. But Pompeianus declined the offer. We do know that Pompeianus twice more rejected imperial titles, once when he was asked by Pertinax—who himself became emperor for a short time—to succeed Commodus and once more when he was asked by Julianus, Pertinax's successor, to become co-emperor. Pompeianus evidently was just not interested in the highest echelons of power, which was probably a wise move considering that Pertinax was killed by his own guard three months after acceding to the throne, while Julianus was betrayed by a soldier after merely two months in power.

Marcus Aurelius was not a sage, but his actions—both as a human being and as emperor—were informed by his practice of Stoicism and his firmly held belief that even small progress was nevertheless progress. As he put it in the *Meditations*, "Labor not as one who is wretched, nor yet as one who would be pitied or admired; but direct your will to one thing only: to act or not to act as social reason requires."[42]

CASE STUDY THREE: JULIAN, THE APOSTATE

A few years ago, I was walking down the Appian Way in Rome. In ancient times, it was a major thoroughfare. It was named after the Roman censor Appius Claudius Caecus; its construction began in 312 BCE, and it eventually connected Rome with the southeast port of Brundisium, modern Brindisi. That particular day was part of "Appian Way Week," during which historians and archaeologists were giving guided tours of the major sites. I took one such tour around the Circus of Maxentius, a complex built by the emperor Maxentius between 306 and 312 CE.

The historian who was giving the tour at some point reminded us that Maxentius famously lost the Battle of the Milvian Bridge on October 28, 312 CE. Maxentius fought that battle against the future emperor Constantine I, who would make Christianity the official state religion and move the capital from Rome to Byzantium (which he promptly renamed Constantinople). I was surprised when she let slip that Maxentius had "unfortunately" lost at the Milvian Bridge. Evidently, seventeen centuries later, some people still feel regret at the shift from paganism to Christianity. That sentiment was much stronger in the immediate aftermath of Constantine's decision, and one of his successors, his nephew Julian, made a last-ditch attempt to reverse the tide. Because he caused so much trouble for the already dominant Christian class, he is now known to us as "the Apostate."

Julian lost most of his family when he was young, courtesy of a killing spree ordered by his cousin, the emperor Constantius II, who wanted to make sure that none of his relatives would get in the way of his power-sharing agreement with his brothers, Constantine II and Constans I (yes, the names are a bit confusing). Julian and his own brother, Gallus, survived because their youth made them seem less of a threat, but just in case, they were excluded from public life and given a strict Christian education. Indeed, for several years, they were both exiled to what amounted to house arrest at an imperial estate in Macellum, Cappadocia, in modern Turkey.

Around age twenty, Julian secretly converted to paganism after having studied Neoplatonism and been influenced by the writings of the philosopher Iamblichus as well as the teachings of the mystic Maximus of Ephesus, who would eventually become Julian's mentor. Here was a member of the imperial family who shied away from politics (by necessity, if nothing else) and embraced philosophical studies, including a stint as a student in Athens.

However, events conspired for Julian to enter politics after all. Constantine II died in 340 CE after having been attacked by his brother Constans, who in turn died ten years later during a conflict with the usurper Magnentius. That left only Constantius II in charge, and he felt that he couldn't control the vast empire by himself. At first he promoted Julian's brother, Gallus, to the rank of caesar, second in command below the imperator.

But Gallus became very unpopular in the provinces that he controlled because of his abusive and tyrannical behavior. He was executed in 354 CE. Now Constantius faced the dilemma of what to do with Julian. He summoned him to the court in Mediolanum (modern Milan) to decide whether to dispatch him or offer him a place in the imperial hierarchy. Thanks in part to the mediation of the empress Eusebia, who was fond of Julian, and to the fact that he was assumed to be a bookish kind of man with his head in the clouds (he was a philosopher, after all!), Julian was spared and in turn was named caesar.

This time, however, Constantius didn't want to make the same mistake he had made with the ambitious Gallus, and he relegated Julian to the troubled province of Gaul, where he was only nominally in charge but in fact acted under the direct supervision of Constantius's field generals. To everyone's surprise, though, Julian gradually asserted himself and ended up scoring a number of impressive military victories against the German tribes that were threatening Roman borders. He even captured King Chnodomarius, the leader of the Alamanni forces, sending him to Constantius in Milan.

Julian also turned out to be a capable and fair administrator, implementing tax reforms to lessen the burden on local populations despite orders to the contrary from the emperor. In a very short period, he was loved by the people and, more consequentially, by the well-trained and battle-tested army of Gaul.

It was at this point that a crisis came. Constantius ordered Julian to send him his best legions so that he could begin a war against the Persians, who had been making trouble down in Mesopotamia. Constantius probably really did need the legions, but he just as likely made the move to weaken Julian, even at the cost of having to face a resurgence of hostility from the always restless German tribes. The problem was that Julian had promised his recruits, all local soldiers, that they wouldn't have to fight outside Gaul. When the order from Constantius was made public the legions rebelled and declared Julian augustus, that is, emperor. Civil war seemed inevitable, with Julian likely to face a much larger army under the command of Constantius. But fate intervened again, and Constantius fell terminally ill while he was on the march. In his testament, he recognized Julian as the only remaining heir to the throne, and so the philosopher became king.

Julian entered Constantinople, acclaimed sole emperor, on December 11, 361. He again proved a capable and fair administrator. He immediately set out to address the widespread corruption at court, firing most previous administrators and promulgating new rules of conduct for their replacements. He reverted to the old custom of emperors behaving as *primus inter pares*, first among equals, and accordingly participated in the sessions of the Senate as a regular member. He expanded the authority of the cities, to the detriment of centralized imperial control, and made the cities' tribute to the imperial coffers voluntary rather than mandatory. While he made a concerted effort to revitalize pagan temples and rituals, he also declared freedom of religion throughout the empire, thus ending the Christian hegemony. However, he prohibited Christian teachers from using classical texts in an effort to thwart their near complete control of schools and their indoctrination of young people.

Julian then spent some time in Antioch, where he clashed with the local Christian authorities. He also tried, somewhat unsuccessfully, to address the corruption of local merchants, who had caused artificial shortages in the supply of grain, nearly starving the city in order to fatten their profits. When his ascetic lifestyle and revival of pagan rituals made him unpopular among the Antiochenes, who were rather libertine in their customs, he wrote a self-mocking satire entitled *Misopogon* (Beard hater), a reference to his own unusual sporting of a beard, in the style of philosophers and predecessors such as Hadrian and Marcus Aurelius.

On March 5, 363 CE, Julian departed from Antioch at the head of an army of eighty thousand to ninety thousand men, heading for Persia to finish what Constantius had started. His campaign against King Shapur II was initially successful, and Julian's army laid siege to the capital city of Ctesiphon. But planned reinforcements failed to materialize, and Julian—still betting on fresh troops to join him—made the mistake of leading his army east, deeper into Persian territory. When it became clear that further progress could not be made, he ordered a retreat through Mesopotamia to the Roman borders. During a Persian attack, however, Julian was wounded in battle and died at the age of thirty-two. Libanius, a friend of Julian, claimed that he had been killed by a Roman spear at the hand of a Christian officer, but the charge was not corroborated by other sources of the time. We will likely never know.

Needless to say, the religious and administrative reforms that Julian had enacted did not have time to take hold, as his successor, the rather inept Jovian, immediately reverted to Christianity as the state religion, a reversal that was confirmed by Jovian's successor, Valentinian I. It is hard to say whether Julian might have succeeded in altering what we now regard as the course of history in that respect. Probably not, as Christianity had already become deeply rooted and because it promised things—such as eternal salvation—that paganism could not. Moreover, paganism itself was never really a religion, as we understand the term, but rather a series of loosely connected social and mystical practices. In the end, the sort of religious tolerance that had made the Roman empire so successful paved the way for the rise of a monotheistic, all-encompassing, exclusivist, and intolerant religion. Once Christianity was established, Roman lenience toward other religious practices went out the window, and eventually so did the empire itself.

Was Julian a good example of a philosopher-king? In many respects, yes. His fight against corruption, his just administration, and his religious tolerance make him one of the best, though short-lived, of the Roman emperors. But he was also rather superstitious, underestimated the opposition that he would face from Christian bishops, and ultimately made a fatal mistake in not aiming for a draw with the Persians. Then again, philosophy doesn't promise to turn us all into sages, only into better human beings. By that standard, Julian the Apostate was indeed a success.

We have now examined a number of examples of philosophers attempting to mold the character of statesmen as well as of statesmen who themselves embraced philosophy as a way of life. The results in both cases were decidedly mixed, at least in the specific instances we considered. It's time to broaden our view and discuss a number of more general approaches to the relationship between philosophy and politics, informed again by our understanding of human character and its perfectibility (or lack thereof). We will begin with the most famous of the ancient Greek treatments of the subject, Plato's *Republic*. We will consider arguably the most infamous of early-modern approaches to the relationship between virtue and political philosophy, that articulated in Machiavelli's *The Prince*. We will then move all the way to our own time to briefly examine some contemporary ideas on the issue. My hope is that the historical-philosophical survey on which we are about to embark will provide us with some understanding of why the virtuous leader is a rare figure indeed.

7

PHILOSOPHY AND POLITICS

Antiphon asked [Socrates]: "How can you suppose that you make politicians of others, when you yourself avoid politics even if you understand them?" "How now, Antiphon?" he retorted, "Should I play a more important part in politics by engaging in them alone or by taking pains to turn out as many competent politicians as possible?"

—XENOPHON, *MEMORABILIA* 1.6.15

PUT THE PHILOSOPHERS IN CHARGE!

A major underlying theme of this book is the relationship, if any, between philosophy and politics, at least as understood in the ancient Western world, though I've repeatedly pointed out that, surprisingly, much of what was evident to Socrates, Thucydides, Plutarch, and others appears—for good or ill—to still be true for us denizens of the twenty-first century.

The other underlying theme is what I have termed the quest for character, which is not confined to the character of leaders but extends to that of every human being who wishes to become a better member of society. The two themes may seem to be only superficially connected, since nowadays we tend to

181

think of personal ethics, and therefore character, as a very distinct matter from social justice and hence politics. I may be a decent person when it comes to how I behave in my private life, but this appears to be largely disconnected from societal issues and particularly from various types of injustice, whether of an economic, racial, or gendered nature. Socrates, Plato & Co. would have been seriously puzzled by this arbitrary demarcation. For them, personal philosophy and politics, as well as character and leadership, were fundamentally inseparable and deeply interconnected. I think they had a point, and it behooves us to consider that point seriously.

One reason for this difference between ancient and modern thought is that the very meaning of the words "philosophy" and "politics" has changed dramatically in the intervening time. I happen to think that it would be a good idea to return to something close to the original. As we noted before, these days a philosopher is someone—like me—who has a PhD in an arcane and highly specialized area of scholarship (in my case, philosophy of science) and who teaches at a university. Mind you, not all modern philosophers are academics, but as a very good first approximation, that picture fits the reality of the situation.

Yet for Socrates or the Stoics, a philosopher was simply someone who attempted to live in a particularly mindful and ethical way. Philosophy was the theory and practice of the art of living, as we have explored in the previous chapter. Cato the Younger, Marcus Aurelius, or Julian the Apostate were philosophers in this sense, not because they spent their lives writing books about metaphysics and whatnot. Socrates, Epicurus, Seneca, Epictetus, and several more were *also* philosophers in the sense of being inquirers, but their inquiries were, again, directed at figuring out better ways for human beings to live, beginning with themselves. A Socrates or Epictetus who preached the eudaimonic life, the life worth living, but didn't actually practice it himself would have been regarded as a fraud (or a Sophist, to use Plato's somewhat unfairly favorite target).

Something similar goes for the word "politics." It is common in contemporary society to hear of people who are not interested in politics or who regard politics as something that doesn't concern them or affect their lives. "Politician" is one of the dirtiest words in the English dictionary, as politicians tend to be consistently ranked among the least trustworthy professionals in poll after poll. But for Aristotle, politics is the study of how to build and maintain a proper polis, that is, a human society. Everyone ought to be interested in this sort of study or—at a minimum— recognize that we are all affected by politics understood in this way for the simple reason that human beings are inherently social animals who live and only thrive in social groups.

From this perspective, it should be easier to grasp why philosophy and politics are inextricably connected: A good polis is one that, ideally, is made of philosophers, or at the very least is guided by philosophers, in the sense of people who wish to live (and govern) virtuously for the benefit of all. This is perhaps nowhere made more clear than in Plato's famous masterpiece, the *Republic*. That book has been much studied, much discussed, and more often than not much misunderstood. Let us take a look at those parts that are most germane to our purposes here.

From a modern perspective, Plato's *kallipolis*—the ideal state—is a veritable mess. It includes elements of socialism since in the book Socrates argues against inequality. It has a flavor of communism since the famous "guardian" class, that is, the philosophers in charge of affairs, will share everything so that they will not be tempted by envy, which means no private property.

There are also clear elements of fascism, for instance, in the censorship of creative works (poetry) so that they will not undermine public morality or in the eugenic program of breeding the best individuals in order to preserve and improve the guardian class. This is no template for any society you or I should want to live in.

But Plato, using Socrates as his main character, explores questions, and offers potential answers, that are still very relevant today. And it is to those questions and possible answers that we turn now. If you are familiar with the *Republic*, you will notice that I will not present things in strict order of appearance across the ten books of Plato's opus. Indeed, I will be skipping over much of what he says and will present the opinions of Socrates and his interlocutors in a nonstandard sequence because that makes more sense to me and hopefully will to you as well.

Readers of the *Republic*, including scholars, are still baffled by what exactly its main topic is supposed to be. Socrates and his friends begin by asking what makes a just person and why anyone would actually want to be just. But then they focus a great part of their inquiry on the structure of the (ideal) just state. So is Plato's text about how to live a eudaimonic life as an individual or about how to build a good society? It is about both, and indeed, in Plato's mind, the second question informs the first one. Strange as it may appear to us, Socrates in the dialogue suggests that if we really want to understand what makes a good human life and a just human being, we need to zoom out, so to speak, and examine what makes a good and just state. Plato, through Platsoc, goes from the microcosm of the human individual to the macrocosm of human society and then back again.

Socrates tells his friends in book II of the *Republic* that the reason we organize ourselves in societies is because we are, by nature, not self-sufficient. Instead, we thrive when we can divide the labors of life among a number of individuals, each of whom will have certain talents that will make him or her best suited to a particular task. Modern science agrees. The species we call *Homo sapiens* evolved in the form of groups of cooperative individuals who are not equipped with any particularly impressive evolutionary weapon. No sharp claws, no powerful muscles, no high-speed running, no flying. What we have, instead, is our ability to reason and our social instincts. We survive and flourish by applying our minds to improving the life of the group and, consequently, our own.

Because we are naturally social animals, we have an instinctive inclination toward "virtue," that is, prosocial behavior. Socrates might have been thinking along these lines when he said, in book IV, that justice is a natural balance of the various parts of the soul, while injustice, correspondingly, is the result of an imbalance among the parts of the soul. We don't have to buy into Plato's specific theory of the soul to consider this notion. Plato thought of the soul as immaterial, immortal, and made of three components: the "rational" part, responsible for our ability to reason; the "spirited" part, where our emotions reside; and the "appetitive" part, where our more animal cravings, for food, drink, and sex, originate. But the Stoics—who thought of themselves as intellectual descendants of Socrates—rejected this tripartition, maintaining instead that the soul is unitary (i.e., not divided into parts), made of matter, and mortal. Regardless, they also understood a good and just person to be internally "balanced," or in harmony with his or her own prosocial human nature, and a bad and unjust person to correspondingly be "imbalanced," or in disharmony.

But why would anyone want to be just, or virtuous, if they can cheat the rest of us and get away with it? In book II of the *Republic*, two of Socrates's friends, Glaucon and Adeimantus (who in real life were both Plato's older brothers), mount a concerted attack on the notion that it is good to be just. Glaucon proposes three arguments in favor of injustice. First, historically, the concept of justice is rooted in the fact that weak people aren't sufficiently bold to take charge of things and are too fearful of the possibility that others will take control, leaving them to suffer the consequences. Second, people tend to act "justly" only because they usually can't get away with doing what they want, that is, out of fear of the consequences of acting unjustly. Finally, maintains Glaucon, a person who is unjust but manages to maintain a reputation for justice is actually happier than one who is truly just but has been tagged with a reputation for injustice.

It is in this context that Glaucon tells the famous story of the ring of Gyges—a story that, incidentally, will provide inspiration to J. R. R. Tolkien for his epic, *The Lord of the Rings*. According to Herodotus in his *Histories*, Gyges of Lydia (modern western Turkey) was a historical king who came to power under suspicious circumstances. The version of the story that we find in Plato's *Republic* is meant to be taken metaphorically. Plato's recounting of the events is far more entertaining than the straightforward historical telling of the betrayal of the king by one of his underlings.

According to Glaucon, one of Gyges's ancestors was a shepherd. One day, in the aftermath of an earthquake, he discovered a hitherto unknown cave and entered it. Inside the cave, he found a tomb with a bronze horse and a corpse. The corpse was wearing a golden ring, which Gyges's ancestor duly pocketed. He soon realized that turning the ring would make him invisible, thus giving him an extraordinary power and a great advantage over his fellow human beings. Did the shepherd use his new powers for the common good, as a modern-day superhero would? Of course not. He headed for the city and, using his invisibility, seduced the queen, killed the king, and made himself monarch. The mythological ancestor of Gyges is invoked by Glaucon to make the point that people do the "right" thing only because they normally lack the power to do otherwise. But give them such power and they will immediately use it. Justice, then, turns out to be a matter of might makes right.

Socrates, in book I of the *Republic*, offers three counterarguments in response to Glaucon's defense of injustice, aiming to establish that a just (or virtuous) life is better than an unjust (or unvirtuous) one. The first argument is that the just person is wise, while the unjust person is ignorant. This may strike us as more than a bit bizarre, since we can all immediately think of a number of bad, unjust individuals who are, however, not at all ignorant. On the contrary, some of the most effective villains of history were both intelligent and educated. But the Greek word that is often translated as "ignorant" really means "lacking wisdom," and since wisdom is a particular kind of knowledge, it follows that when one lacks it, one is, in effect, "ignorant." This is the same crucial aspect of Socratic (and Stoic) philosophy that we encountered at the beginning of this book when we looked at the dialogues between Socrates and Alcibiades.

Socrates's second counterargument is that injustice produces internal disharmony, which in turn has the consequence of rendering one's actions ineffective. This is at least in part an empirical argument, and accordingly it stands or falls on the basis of evidence. Modern research in social psychology does tend to confirm that most people think of themselves as essentially good, and that when they are confronted with evidence of their own ill behavior, they experience cognitive dissonance, an un-pleasant psychological sensation generated by a strident contrast between two notions we happen to hold or between a notion we entertain and some evidence contrary to it.[1] We could reason-ably call cognitive dissonance a type of internal "disharmony." We may further suggest that the reason we want to think of ourselves as good is a joint result of cultural pressures and our fundamental instincts as prosocial primates. If this makes sense, then Socrates was really not far off the mark when he suggested that bad behavior causes what we would think of as psychic im-balances in a human being.

The third Socratic counterargument is also intriguing and also arguably supported by contemporary scientific evidence. He says that virtue (*arete* in Greek) is excellence at the proper function of someone or something. We have seen earlier that we can meaningfully talk, for instance, of an excellent knife, meaning a knife that is very good at what knives are supposed to do, cutting things. Something similar goes for living beings as well. A cactus, for instance, excels at living in dry environ-ments with a lot of sunlight and little water. That is, as we now know, because the cactus evolved to survive and thrive in such environments, which are not friendly to other life forms, in-cluding many plants. Similarly, a human being is by nature a social animal capable of reasoning, as we have also seen before. So an excellent human being is one who uses reason correctly and who lives in a prosocial (i.e., "virtuous") manner. The just, good, prosocial person, therefore, is actually happier than the unjust, bad, antisocial one because the first, but not the second, approximates *arete* for a human being.

In book IX of the *Republic*, Socrates advances yet another argument in favor of the person who is just and pursues the philosophical life, an argument aimed at establishing that this is the kind of person whom we want to trust and, in fact, emulate. Broadly speaking, says Socrates, there are three types of people in the world: those who pursue wisdom, or the philosophical life; those who pursue honor (soldiers, athletes, wannabe celebrities); and those whose chief goal is profit (merchants, businesspeople). Which life is more pleasant or more conducive to happiness? He concludes that we should listen to what the philosophers have to say on the grounds that they alone are most clearly capable of considering and comparing all three lifestyles. That's why philosophers—again, understood not as professional academics but as pursuers of wisdom—should be in charge of the *kallipolis*. I doubt that many today will find Socrates's argument persuasive, but it does anticipate a similar one put forth during the nineteenth century by John Stuart Mill.

Mill was faced with a different problem. He was a pupil of Jeremy Bentham, the founder of Utilitarianism, an important framework for modern ethics. Utilitarians maintain that whatever increases most people's happiness is good, and whatever diminishes most people's happiness is bad, making Utilitarianism the chief modern hedonistic philosophy. The problem is, as Mill immediately realized, that there are some nefarious consequences to the sort of simplistic "hedonic calculus" that Bentham advocated. It may turn out, for instance, that what makes most people happy is to watch reality TV all day while eating junk food. Utilitarianism would then push the world toward the minimum common denominator in terms of how human beings spend their time. To avoid this, Mill qualitatively distinguished between "lower" (physical) pleasures and "higher" (mental, moral) pleasures, giving more weight to the latter than the former (though the lower pleasures are still part of a balanced life). All right, but who establishes what counts as a lower or higher pleasure? Those people, answers Mill, who are capable of experiencing and evaluating both. As he rather sarcastically puts it in his book *Utilitarianism*, "It is better to be a human being dissatisfied than a pig satisfied; better to be Socrates dissatisfied than a fool satisfied. And if the fool, or the pig, are of a different opinion, it is because they only know their own side of the question."[2]

Both Mill and Socrates strike us as insufferably elitist, of course. But elitism is a bad thing only when it is an excuse for oppressing people and privileging the few. We don't have a problem with excellent doctors, athletes, businesspeople, and so forth being recognized as the best at what they do. Nor do we have any trouble accepting their opinions or respecting their achievements in their proper areas of expertise. So why have a problem with philosophers—that is, people who pursue wisdom and practice virtue—being in charge of realizing a wise and virtuous society? They clearly are the best for the job.

MIGHT MAKES RIGHT, RIGHT?

Ever since, and in fact even before, Socrates and Plato, there has always been a second approach—other than one based on seeking justice—to running a polis, the sort of take we have seen defended by Glaucon: "Right" is really a nice way to say "might." Accordingly, we should do things along the lines of what has become known as realpolitik, from the German for practical politics. The idea is that statesmen should act on the basis of prudential factors reflecting the circumstances on the ground, rather than on the basis of moral principles, and that the raison d'être of a state is not the happiness of its citizens but only their security and material prosperity.

Realpolitik is nowadays formalized in the general approach known as political realism, which applies not just at the national level but also at the level of international relations. We have now moved from the small scale city-states Plato was familiar with to the global stage where leaders of nations numbering tens or hundreds of millions of people operate.

A basic idea of political realism is that the world will always, indeed necessarily, be characterized by conflict. The reasons adduced by realists vary from the alleged fundamental selfishness embedded in human nature to the absence, so far, of a supranational authority that would be able to prevent or suppress conflict (the way the police are supposed to do within a state). Of course these sorts of explanations aren't mutually exclusive.

Modern political realism hinges on four fundamental theses. First, states—not national leaders or international organizations such as the UN—are the central actors on the world stage. Second, at the global level, nation-states form an essentially anarchic group in which international law is largely ignored unless it serves a given state's interests at the moment. Third, states, as individual agents, operate in a manner analogous to what in economics is called rational self-interest. Finally, states pursue self-preservation through the acquisition of as much power as their resources allow. As you can see, this is a rather bleak view of humanity and human relations, and the word "ethics" is nowhere to be found.

Political realism has a long history in both the East and the West. In the Eastern tradition, it allegedly goes back to the famous *Art of War*, attributed to the fifth-century BCE author Sun Tzu. The book is fundamentally about military strategy, yet it has been touted as a guide to international relations in the realist tradition, as well as to business practices, because most of the advice contained in it is actually about how to obtain an advantage while avoiding direct confrontation. *The Art of War* is recommended reading for all US military intelligence personnel, and even the fictional Captain Picard of *Star Trek* at one point expresses satisfaction that Sun Tzu is still read at Starfleet Academy.[3]

In the Western tradition, political realism claims none other than Thucydides as its forerunner. This connection, however, is more complex than it may at first appear since Thucydides actually peppers his *History of the Peloponnesian War* with moral judgments and is in fact particularly harsh toward his fellow Athenians. True, Thucydides set himself the task of describing events dispassionately and of reconstructing the causes of the war as well as of its individual episodes as scientifically as possible. But he also made it very clear that he believed that the disaster that had befallen the Athenians was, in no small part, the result of their own moral failings.

The real unquestioned predecessor of early political realism, however, is the Italian Niccolò Machiavelli. Opinions about his famous short treatise on practical politics, *The Prince*, have varied enormously since its posthumous publication in 1532. It circulated freely for a while, but it was added to the Index of Prohibited Books by Pope Paul IV in 1559, apparently at the prompting of Cardinal Reginald Pole, who said that the book had been written by Satan's finger.

Even in modern times, no less than an authority on the history of philosophy than Bertrand Russell said that *The Prince* is a handbook for gangsters. Sure enough, Mussolini used it as a practical guide for twentieth-century politics. Not every philosopher, however, has held the book in such contempt as Russell did. Jean-Jacques Rousseau was of the opinion that the little treatise was itself a Machiavellian trick, so to speak: It pretended to be addressed to the princes of Italy, but it was a covert manual for revolutionary action on the part of the people. It takes a bit too much optimism to agree with Rousseau here, but it is undoubtedly the case that Russell also was completely off the mark. *The Prince* is what it claims to be: a detached analysis, based on historical examples, of the dynamics of power and, especially, of how power can be acquired and retained.

The reason that Machiavelli is justly seen as the precursor of political realism is not that he was devious and preached deceit but that he saw clearly through the hypocrisy of the rulers whom he observed at close range. One pope after another, as well as one member of the Medici family in Florence after another, kept talking about the Christian virtues that allegedly moved them and that guided their actions and yet behaved ruthlessly and decidedly unvirtuously. If you actually read *The Prince*, you will indeed find counsel to lie in order to maintain power but also the recognition that—ultimately—power rests with the people (because there are more of them) and that therefore no leader can survive long if he does not act in the interests of the people. Just ask Mussolini.

Machiavelli wrote *The Prince* when he was forty-four years old and his diplomatic career was, temporarily, as it turns out, in ruins. He had successfully served as the chief diplomat of the Republic of Florence for fourteen years, but a change in the political winds led to a suspicion that he was conspiring against the new government, headed by the reestablished Medici family. He was put into prison and tortured but continued to deny any disloyalty. He was released and went into exile in the countryside, where he wrote *The Prince*. The question that exercised his mind was how to win and retain power in a world that functions

as a result of cause and effect (not divine will), where survival—
of both the individual and the state—is paramount and everything else, especially talk of virtue and justice, is a luxury that
few can afford.

Machiavelli's thinking was of course influenced not just by
his direct experience of politics but also by the fascinating times
during which he grew up. He observed that there was a radical
disconnect between how those in power described what they
were doing and the actual way in which they acted, apparently
moved by very different internal forces than those they publicly
declared. Let us not forget that the Renaissance was the time
when popes rode their horses into battle. In Florence itself, one
of the beacons of the Italian Renaissance, the republican constitution (i.e., the theory) was highly idealistic, but the place was
for all effective purposes a small oligarchy run by the Medici
family (i.e., the practice).

When Machiavelli was about to turn nine years old in 1478,
a group of conspirators against Medici power, members of the
Pazzi family, were hung from the windows of the main government building and left to rot for days as an example to would-be
challengers. We can imagine how such a view made an impres-
sion on the very young Niccolò, perhaps later spurring his re-
flections on the highly personal cost of failure in politics. Then
again, there were also unexpectedly high payoffs, such as when
Lorenzo de' Medici managed to charm the pope enough to have
his thirteen-year-old nephew made cardinal. Lorenzo went
from being excommunicated to being a favorite of the pontifex,
quite a reversal of fortune engineered by his diplomatic skills,
backed by the economic and military power of Florence.

Machiavelli was elected to one of the most important posts
in the city government shortly after the downfall of another

larger-than-life figure, Girolamo Savonarola, a Dominican friar who temporarily turned Florence into a fundamentalist theocracy (complete with book-burning parties) from 1494 to 1498. Finally the pope was able to sufficiently undermine Savonarola's power base, convict him of heresy, and burn him at the stake. Again, this must have taught the young diplomat an important lesson.

In 1502, four years into his job and now thirty-three years old, Machiavelli was on a diplomatic mission that would further sharpen his sense of how politics worked in practice, reinforcing the notion that might, within limits, really does make right. It was then that he met Cesare Borgia, the son of Pope Alexander VI and one of Italy's rising stars as a *condottiere*, that is, captain of (usually mercenary) armies. Borgia had laid siege to and captured the city of Urbino, not far from Florence, and made it the starting point for his own territorial expansion with the blessing of his "holy" father. Machiavelli's mission was, for all effective purposes, to dissuade Borgia from marching on Florence, and he succeeded.

The following year, on another mission to see the *condottiere*, Machiavelli learned a thing or two about the modus operandi of the man he at one point considered Italy's best hope against the scourge of foreign (i.e., French and Spanish) invasion. Borgia was running into problems with some noblemen of a nearby town, belonging to the Orsini family, who weren't too happy about his plans for expansion. They were invited by Borgia to the city of Senigallia, allegedly to conduct peace talks and reach a reciprocally suitable agreement. Instead they were captured as soon as they set foot inside the walls and then executed. You can call it diplomacy Italian style, circa 1500 CE. Machiavelli later wrote that the prince sometimes must use such obviously unvirtuous means to hold on to power. If he succeeds, the people will soon forget the cruelty and will not hold him accountable. Political leaders are—practically speaking—above the law so long as they keep delivering.

Another illustrative episode took place in the Borgia-occupied city of Cesena, a territory that needed to be "pacified." I will let Machiavelli himself tell the story: "He appointed Remirro de Orco, a cruel, no-nonsense man, and gave him complete control. In a short while de Orco pacified and united the area.... As soon as he found a pretext, he had de Orco beheaded and his corpse put on display one morning in the piazza in Cesena with a wooden block and a bloody knife beside. The ferocity of the spectacle left people both gratified and shocked."[4] Borgia had one of his henchmen do the dirty job on his behalf, knowing that this would anger the people. Since a prince needs the support of the population, Borgia found an excuse to accuse and convict de Orco, thus both giving the people what they wanted and deflecting their ire from his own person.

But Cesare Borgia's luck ran out in 1503, when both he and his father fell ill. Alexander died, thus depriving his son of much-needed political and military support. The lesson that Machiavelli learned from this particular episode is that daring, cunning, and ruthlessness will only get you so far. Luck—what the Stoics referred to as the universal web of cause and effect—cannot be counted on, and a wise person ought to be prepared for even the best plans to be ruined by the mysterious workings of the universe.

This was confirmed to Machiavelli not just by his observations of the rise and fall of various political figures in Italy but by his own personal story. In 1512, the new pope, Julius II, backed the Medicis and helped them defeat the Florentine forces at

Prato. The truly virtuous, but not very bold, leader of Florence, Piero Soderini, capitulated and went into exile. As a side product of these events, Machiavelli was now out of a job. It was in the aftermath of this downfall that he wrote *The Prince*, which he dedicated first to Giuliano Medici and eventually to the family member who really held power, Giuliano's nephew Lorenzo (known as Lorenzo II to distinguish him from his more illustrious predecessor, Lorenzo the Magnificent). There is no evidence that Lorenzo ever opened the book, which circulated in manuscript form until after Machiavelli's death.

Understandably, Machiavelli was disappointed by the poor reception of what he considered his ticket back into the halls of Florentine power. He therefore turned to a couple of his other talents. One was womanizing and the other, related, was writing comedies centered on sex. The staging of his first play, *The Mandragola*, in 1518 made him an instant celebrity. It's the story of a young man who comes up with absurd plans in order to get the object of his lust, a married young woman, into bed. This was followed a few years later by *Clizia*, another successful play in which an old man becomes very creative in pursuing his goal of seducing a younger woman. But Machiavelli's heart was in politics, as he wrote to a friend, Francesco Vettori:

When evening comes, I go back home, and go to my study. On the threshold, I take off my work clothes, covered in mud and filth, and I put on the clothes an ambassador would wear. Decently dressed, I enter the ancient courts of rulers who have long since died. There, I am warmly welcomed, and I feed on the only food I find nourishing and was born to savor. I am not ashamed to talk to them and ask them to explain their actions and they, out of kindness, answer me. Four hours go by without my feeling any anxiety. I forget every worry. I am no longer afraid of poverty or frightened of death. I live entirely through them.[5]

He did briefly have a second chance thanks to yet another pope, Clement VII, also known as Giulio de' Medici—the guy who commissioned Michelangelo to paint the ceiling of the Sistine Chapel. Giulio wanted Machiavelli's advice on a matter that was becoming increasingly urgent in Italian affairs: how to deal with the antagonism between Spain and France, which was being played out on the Italian peninsula. Unfortunately for both Giulio and Machiavelli, the Spanish army marched on Rome and sacked it on May 6, 1527. Shortly thereafter, Florence fell too, and the Medici regime collapsed again, putting Machiavelli permanently out of a job. He did not recover from the blow. Perhaps in part because he insisted on taking dubious medications, he died later that same year at the age of fifty-eight.

The Prince became both a point of reference and a reviled book, so much so that today the term "Machiavellian" is still usually not meant as a compliment. As Tim Parks, in his introduction to the Penguin translation of the book, aptly puts it, "Machiavelli's little book was a constant threat. It reminded people that power is always up for grabs, always a question of what can be taken by force or treachery, and always, despite all protests to the contrary, the prime concern of any ruler."[6]

Since Machiavelli, political realism has seen a number of major theoretical developments and practitioners. Indubitably the most influential early philosopher in this vein was Thomas Hobbes, whose *Leviathan, or The Matter, Forme and Power of a Commonwealth Ecclesiasticall and Civil*, articulated the need for a strong ruler in order to avoid the state of nature to which—according to Hobbes—we would otherwise inevitably revert, a state famously characterized in the book as a war of all against all: "In such condition there is no place for industry, because the fruit thereof is uncertain, and consequently no culture of the earth, no navigation nor the use of commodities that may be imported by sea, no commodious building, no instruments of moving and removing such things as require much force, no knowledge of the face of the earth, no account of time, no arts, no letters, no society, and which is worst of all, continual fear and danger of violent death, and the life of man, solitary, poor, nasty, brutish, and short."[7]

Well, who wouldn't give up all liberties in order to avoid *that*? Among the practitioners of Machiavellianism, as one might fairly label the approach, is a who's who of early-modern and contemporary statesmen, from the French Cardinal Richelieu (of *Three Musketeers* fame) to the Prussian monarch Frederick the Great, from the Italian Camillo Benso of Cavour to another Prussian, Otto von Bismarck, and all the way down to Mao Zedong, Charles de Gaulle, and Henry Kissinger.

Contemporary political scientists recognize four successive versions of realism. So-called classical realism is a direct descendant of Hobbes's (and Machiavelli's) views and assumes that it is simply in the nature of human beings, and by extension of states, to seek power in the service of self-preservation, above and beyond any officially professed ideology. According to a second school, known as neorealism, international dynamics are driven by the fact that states operate, for all intents and purposes, in an anarchic environment, given the absence of effective supranational organizations (the UN not being nearly enough). While "liberal" realists, the third school, acknowledge the essentially anarchic international milieu, they nevertheless maintain that there still exists an informal society of states that follow norms aimed at blunting the degree of anarchism. Finally, the fourth school, neoclassical realism, arches back again to Machiavelli and Hobbes in an attempt to ameliorate the perceived short-comings of neorealism, especially its inability to account for the behavior of particular states.

Regardless of the flavor of political realism one may be considering, the fact is that all of its forms, both historical and present, have a distinctly antidemocratic, and often imperialistic, tone. Are there alternatives?

AGAINST REALPOLITIK: POLITICAL LIBERALISM AND ETHICAL PRAGMATISM

The standard modern response to political realism is often referred to as liberalism. Like political realism, it has deep philosophical roots, in this case going back to the major thinkers of the Enlightenment, including John Locke, Voltaire, and Immanuel Kant. Locke's *Two Treatises of Government*, published in 1689, and Kant's *To Perpetual Peace: A Philosophical Sketch*, published in 1795, are crucial points of reference.

Locke's *Two Treatises* assume that human beings are born as blank slates (tabula rasa) with no innate ideas, an assumption that has certainly not held up well given the subsequent developments of evolutionary biology and cognitive science. Nevertheless, the notion is that the state of nature is one of anarchy, which can be ameliorated only by the establishment of a civic government. People will then act more rationally, simply because the government imposes laws and there are consequences for violating those laws. Crucially, governments grant rights, including the fundamental ones of life, liberty, and property.

These are the ideas that shaped the thinking of the founding fathers of the United States and that spurred the American and French revolutions.

Kant's essay was the first to propose that the best route to international peace is the spread of democracy on the (alleged) ground that democracies will not fight wars, since conflict will be unpopular and democratic leaders will be held accountable at the voting booth. Moreover, increasingly intertwined economic relationships will also make it less likely that countries will go to war because everybody would lose out in the ensuing conflict. These ideas—like Locke's tabula rasa—have also not withstood the test of time particularly well, and modern liberals have conceded that democracies do, in fact, wage war. However, current thinking is that democratic nations are extremely unlikely to fight wars *against each other* since each potential combatant's citizens will likely see the citizens of other democratic nations as endorsing the same values. That, it must be said, certainly is not the way things worked out during the Peloponnesian War.

Contemporary liberalism rejects the idea, basic to political realism, that power is central to international relations, shifting the emphasis instead to the mutual benefits of cooperation. While realism denies any significant role for international and nongovernmental organizations, these are central to the liberal approach, particularly the United Nations and the European Union but also international military alliances such as the North Atlantic Treaty Organization (NATO) and nongovernmental organizations such as the World Bank. International trade and the spread of democracy are still seen as pivotal factors in maintaining peace. Liberalism further rejects the realist notion that international relations are a zero-sum game, shifting the focus from relative gains to absolute gains: Everyone gets better because of enhanced cooperation and reduced conflict.

Two further pillars of modern liberalism are the importance of international law and the aspirational guidance offered by the concept of cosmopolitanism. These two notions bring us back full circle to the beginning of our inquiry. Ancient Greece was certainly, in many respects, a very different place from the modern world stage. But the Greeks did have the notion of "international" law, and they had their own version of "cosmopolitanism," often referred to as Panhellenism. One of the main lessons that one learns from Thucydides is that things went well for the Greek city-states precisely when they managed to transcend local rivalries, coalescing together into a Panhellenic league. That is, after all, how they repeatedly defeated the mighty Persians. Moreover, the times of peace and prosperity that punctuated the Peloponnesian War took place precisely when Athens, Sparta, and their respective allies agreed to respect the ancient equivalent of international law—that is, the commonly understood practices of inter-polis relationships outside periods of warfare.

The Stoics, taking a cue from Socrates and a hand from the Cynics, made true cosmopolitanism—that is, not just Panhellenism—one of the centerpieces of their philosophy. As Epictetus puts it, "Do as Socrates did, never replying to the question of where he was from with, 'I am Athenian,' or 'I am from Corinth,' but always, 'I am a citizen of the world.'"[8]

While the Cynic and early Stoic versions of cosmopolitanism were an abstract ideal that likely nobody seriously thought would ever be realized, the Academic Skeptic Cicero—influenced by the Stoics—began to articulate a political program that relied on precisely the connection between philosophy and politics that Socrates tried to inculcate (unsuccessfully, as we've seen) in Alcibiades: At least those who rule and write the laws ought to practice virtue (though ideally, of course, everyone should). Marcus Aurelius is perhaps the best example of what they might have had in mind: a ruler and general who was also a philosopher in the sense of a practitioner of the art of living. Someone who had at heart the good of both the people he was leading and the human cosmopolis in general. And this was something Marcus explicitly set himself to as a standard: "My city and country, so far as I am Antoninus, is Rome; but so far as I am a man, it is the world."[9]

Marcus tried to put these principles into practice, at least as much as he could given the circumstances and the culture in which he lived and operated. He did not, for instance, fight wars of expansion but only of defense of the existing borders of the Roman Empire. Moreover, he attempted repeatedly to negotiate mutually beneficial solutions with the German tribes on the northern border rather than resort to violence, and even when he had to fight, he resettled large numbers of former enemy soldiers within Roman territory rather than go the usual route often practiced, for instance, by the Athenians, that is, a combination of genocide and enslavement.

We moderns tend to underestimate the role of character in our leaders and to overestimate the functionality of our institutions. We are proud of our national constitutions and, at least some of us, of international laws. But the ancients, especially the Romans, understood very well that no system, regardless of how good it is in principle, will lead to a just and peaceful society unless people—beginning with those in charge—act in a somewhat virtuous fashion. The Romans referred to the concept of *mos maiorum*, often translated as "the way of the ancestors." The idea was that a society functions only insofar as its members and leaders follow accepted principles, models of behavior, and social practices. The *mos maiorum* was understood as dynamically complementary with a society's laws. If the *mos maiorum* breaks down, then there is no system of law that is sufficiently resilient to guarantee a functional society. According to Cicero, it was the increasingly evident breakdown of the *mos maiorum* that was leading (and did lead, shortly after his death) to the collapse of the Roman Republic.

When Julius Caesar defied the *mos maiorum* and entered Italy—crossing the Rubicon at the head of one of his legions— he was doing something unprecedented, breaking all rules of conduct and declaring war against the Senate, for all effective purposes opening the way to further acts of defiance that eventually led to the destruction of the Republic and the beginning of the Empire. We are seeing something like the collapse of *mos maiorum* happening in modern times, not only in so-called failed states but in allegedly functional democracies such as the United States. When a political appointee under investigation for corruption unilaterally decides, for instance, to ignore the subpoena served to him by Congress or when a political party actively works toward voter suppression in order to gain an unfair advantage in the next election, they are violating the *mos maiorum* and paving the way for possible chaos and civil war—or tyranny. As it happened in Rome more than two millennia ago.

This is why a good constitution and good legislation are necessary but not sufficient elements of a good society. We also need individuals who actively try to better themselves, that is, to practice virtue. Politics, in other words, needs philosophy and cannot be done in the Machiavellian "realist" tradition. That said, the liberal model is also clearly deficient because—as

Glaucon never tires of reminding Socrates in the *Republic*—we still need to reckon with the indubitable lure of might.

There is, as it turns out, a third way between realism and liberalism that does not discount the existence and exercise of force and at the same time calls for an ethical approach to societal affairs and international politics. I am referring to the real realpolitik, as originally conceptualized by Ludwig von Rochau in his 1853 book, *Principles of Realpolitik Applied to the National State of Affairs of Germany.* He wrote,

> The study of the forces that shape, maintain and alter the state is the basis of all political insight and leads to the understanding that the law of power governs the world of states just as the law of gravity governs the physical world. The older political science was fully aware of this truth but drew a wrong and detrimental conclusion—the right of the more powerful. The modern era has corrected this unethical fallacy, but while breaking with the alleged right of the more powerful one, the modern era was too much inclined to overlook the real might of the more powerful and the inevitability of its political influence.[10]

Von Rochau was writing in the aftermath of two momentous periods in European history: the Enlightenment and the revolutions of 1848. The Enlightenment had inspired the revolutions in America and France, the former a success, the latter a failure. But it had also led to revolts against tyranny and absolute rule that shook Europe in 1848. They spread like wildfire: Denmark, France, the German states, Ireland, Italy, Spain, Sweden, Switzerland, and so forth, overall affecting more than fifty countries. Most of these movements were violently suppressed, with tens of thousands of people dying. The liberal cry for reform, democracy, and justice had led the way, but the reactionary use of force had ultimately carried the day. At least temporarily. The mind is tempted to draw a parallel with the failed Arab Spring movements of the early 2010s.

The lesson that von Rochau took from all of this is that positive change must be guided by the right ethical compass, but it is naive and dangerous to think that one can achieve lasting results just by politely asking the powers that be to please step aside. Again, we have seen this truth unfolding before our eyes in the case of the contemporary movements for social justice in the United States and in other countries.

Plato thought that the answer was to put "philosophers" in charge. Socrates, similarly, argued that whoever is at the helm of a society ought to be virtuous or disaster will ensue. The Stoics thought that, in fact, we need to work toward a society where everyone is dedicated to the practice of virtue, and in that society we will, finally, not need laws or weapons. But what do we do in the meantime? We work with what we have, attempting to improve things and avoid backsliding, always guided by the light of reason and virtue. As Marcus Aurelius, the Roman emperor who came closest to our model of a philosopher and statesman, put it, "Set yourself in motion, if it is in your power, and do not look about you to see if anyone will observe it; nor yet expect Plato's *Republic*: but be content if the smallest thing goes on well, and consider such an event to be no small matter."[11]

Speaking of not waiting for Plato's *Republic*, that is, for utopia, most of us are unlikely to have a chance to tutor the next Alexander or Marcus, though—at least in more or less democratic countries—we have a chance to elect people of good character. Meanwhile, it is incumbent on us to improve our own character and to influence that of the people who are close to us, beginning with our relatives and friends. But how do we do that? In the final chapter, we will take a look at what does and does not work when it comes to becoming better human beings, arguably the most consequential contribution each and every one of us can make to eventually build a better world.

8

IT'S ALL ABOUT CHARACTER

Fortune has no jurisdiction over character.

—SENECA, LETTER XXXVI.6

THE EMPIRICAL EVIDENCE

Much of what we have implicitly, and sometimes explicitly, been discussing so far has to do with character. The people we have encountered who were trying their best to do some good—from Socrates to Marcus Aurelius and from Cato to Julian—could fairly be described as having had a good character. By contrast, the problematic people in our story—from Alcibiades to Dionysius I and Dionysius II to Nero—could just as fairly be described as having had a bad character.

But what, exactly, *is* "character"? What evidence do we have that it even exists? Why should we focus on character when we talk about politics? Or about our own life, for that matter? And what does philosophy have to do with it? Let's begin with the basic question: What is character? Christian Miller, one of the most astute modern students of character in all its aspects,[1] has done a lot of thinking and research on the topic, and I shall follow his lead throughout this discussion.

Miller asks us to consider someone we truly like and respect (say, a good friend) and then compare that person to someone we truly despise (say, Joseph Stalin). If we were to describe these two people to explain why we like or dislike them, what would we say? We would likely describe their character. Your friend may be trustworthy and kind. Stalin, by contrast, was cruel, heartless, insensitive, brutal, and ruthless.

The term "character" indicates a lot of other aspects of our personality, not just the morally salient ones (e.g., one can be an introvert or an extrovert), but our focus here is on the moral dimension. Ever since Plato and Aristotle, moral character traits have been organized into two opposing groups: virtues and vices. Plato famously recognized four cardinal virtues, later inherited by the Stoics: practical wisdom (knowledge of how to best navigate complex situations), courage (in the moral sense), justice (conceived as fairness and respect), and temperance (i.e., self-control). If one lacks these virtues, then one is affected by the corresponding vices: unwisdom, cowardice, injustice, and intemperance.

Predictably, different cultures value different combinations of virtues and condemn different kinds of vices. However, you may remember a cross-cultural comparison I mentioned at the beginning of the book, carried out by Katherine Dahlsgaard and collaborators,[2] which revealed a consistent pattern of core virtues that pop up in most, if not all, literate cultures. Specifically, the research compared the concept of virtue across major traditions such as Confucianism, Daoism, Buddhism, Hinduism, "Athenian philosophy" (mostly Plato and Aristotle), Christianity, Judaism, and Islam.

The six "core virtues" identified across these traditions are courage, justice, humanity, temperance, wisdom, and transcendence. They are described in the following manner:

Courage: Emotional strength that involves the exercise of will to accomplish goals in the face of internal or external opposition; specific manifestations include bravery, perseverance, and authenticity (honesty).

Justice: Civic-minded strength that makes healthy community life possible; it includes fairness, leadership, and citizenship or teamwork.

Humanity: Interpersonal strength that involves "tending and befriending" others; it includes intentional acts of love and kindness.

Temperance: Strength that protects against excess; manifestations comprise forgiveness, humility, prudence, and self-control.

Wisdom: Cognitive strength that entails the acquisition and use of knowledge; it includes creativity, curiosity, judgment, perspective, and the ability to provide counsel to others.

Transcendence: Strength derived from cultivating connections to the larger universe that provides personal meaning; it manifests itself as gratitude, hope, and spirituality.

It seems, therefore, that people across the planet—regardless of cultural background—not only think there is such a thing as character but, in the moral realm, at least, value more or less the same set of positive character attributes, or virtues.

But how can we tell whether a person is virtuous? Miller invites us to consider the case of compassion. If our imaginary friend Maria performs one compassionate action—say, she makes a donation to a charity—that's not enough to conclude that she is a compassionate person. She could have done that single thing for a number of reasons, from losing a bet with a friend to showing off. Moreover, much hinges on how an action is performed. Does she act with proper humility or ostentatiously?

So we need to establish a *pattern* of virtuous behavior under a wide range of circumstances before we can feel comfortable saying that Maria is, in fact, a compassionate person. An important point to consider is that if motivations enter into the picture, then it will be somewhat difficult to establish whether a person is virtuous since we usually can only observe what people do, without having access to their internal mental states and therefore to the motives behind their actions. Besides, some of those motives may be opaque to the people themselves. Introspection is a notoriously tricky business.

Nevertheless, once a pattern of virtuous behavior is established, the virtuous character tends to be stable. If your friend is trustworthy, she will be so for extended periods of time and under a variety of specific circumstances. A similar analysis applies to the vices. Unvirtuous people are not easy to detect on the basis of single instances or narrow circumstances. For instance, someone might get a kick out of inflicting pain on animals, but he abstains from doing so to the neighbor's dog for fear of being caught. He may, therefore, develop a good reputation, even though his character is vicious. Miller reminds us of what H. Jackson Brown, the author of *Life's Little Instruction Book*, said about this: "Character is what we do when we think no one is looking."[3] Brown's warning applies particularly to our assessment of politicians, who distressingly often are able to fool a lot of people for a long time, though occasionally we catch them doing something apparently "out of character," which, it turns out, is actually revelatory of their true character.

Miller's fundamental thesis is that there seems to be a gap between how good we would like to be (or even think we are) and the real us. As we have seen at the beginning of this book, this was certainly the case for Alcibiades, and in this respect, he turns out to be anything but exceptional. A more or less large character gap is found in most people, as is evidenced by plenty of solid empirical evidence. Miller calls his generic human being—the aggregate of all the experiments he has examined—Frank. The good news is that Frank is in the company of 76 percent of people when he voluntarily helps someone he has never met before out of empathy for the stranger's predicament. He is also unwilling to cheat if he is reminded of his values, and that holds even when no one is watching.[4]

Then again, Frank is a common victim of the bystander effect:[5] if someone is in need of assistance, he won't help if he happens to be surrounded by people who are not helping. It's not that Frank has now suddenly turned into a vicious person. He is simply unsure what to do and does not want to risk the embarrassment of standing out, especially if it turns out that he has somehow misread the situation.

Studies show that Frank—and hence most of us—is all over the map: Sometimes he behaves admirably, other times despicably. Moreover, these changes are extremely sensitive to our surroundings, often in ways that we don't consciously appreciate. For example, people are more likely to help strangers if they have just passed a bakery from which a warm and pleasant odor of bread or pastries is emanating! This particular effect is strong, with controls helping 22 percent (males) and 17 percent (females) of the time, contrasted with bakery-triggered subjects helping 45 percent (males) and 61 percent (females) of the time.[6] I guess one way to make the world a better place is to start baking bread in every neighborhood!

This research has another disturbing implication: We often don't know our own motivations for helping or not helping. We are usually not conscious of the bystander or bakery effects, and if we do or do not act on a given occasion and are then asked about why we did or didn't, we are likely to come up with reasons that have, in fact, little to do with the actual causal web. We confabulate, as psychologists say.

More generally, Miller argues on the basis of his comparative research that we behave as a result of a mix of attitudes, which include egoistic ones, when we are concerned about feeling or looking better in front of others; duties, when we help others out of a sense of responsibility but not genuine care; and true altruism, when our concern really is focused primarily on the other person. Because of this, we should be careful when we say that someone has a generous or a vicious character since most people oscillate between generosity and viciousness, depending on the circumstances. Most of us, like Frank, fall somewhere in the (dynamic) middle.

We have a natural tendency to infer character from individual actions, but since actions can take different moral valence depending on the situation, such an inference (from "She donated money to a charity" to "She is a generous person") is often unwarranted. That said, we don't behave randomly either. Indeed, our behavior is very reliably predictable under similar circumstances. According to Miller, "how aggressive Frank is when he is in one...situation (for instance, the bar) is very similar to how aggressive he is the next time he is in the same situation (the bar, a week later). This is true despite the fact that Frank behaves so differently from one situation (the bar) to the next (when he is cut off in traffic)."[7] Practically speaking, then, we should lower our generalized expectations about people's moral character. Conversely, those expectations should be raised under the right environmental circumstances: Moral reminders, inducements for enhanced empathy, or good-smelling bread all reliably augment the chances that someone will behave virtuously.

So far we have seen that human beings tend to value more or less the same small set of character traits, or virtues. However, it also turns out that there usually is a "gap" between where we'd like to be, character-wise, and where we actually are. The obvious question, then, is how do we close the character gap? Miller contends, data in hand, that three common strategies don't, in fact, work: do nothing, virtue labeling, and nudging.

You may not be terribly surprised to find out that **doing nothing** (the first strategy) doesn't help, but in fact, that conclusion is not as obvious as it may at first appear. The idea of the doing-nothing strategy is that our character improves naturally while aging, simply because we accumulate life experiences and mature in the process. Indeed, there is some empirical evidence that traits such as conscientiousness do change and get better with age. The problem is that at the same time, the older we get, the more set in our ways we get, with the chances of real improvement becoming smaller and smaller. More generally, we have pretty good evidence from a number of other domains that we hardly achieve excellence at something by not actively working at it, and since we begin life with a fairly large gap between where our characters are and where they should be, doing nothing doesn't seem a good way to go.

The second strategy that doesn't work very well is **virtue labeling**, where we go around referring to people as honest, conscientious, and so forth, even when they are not, hoping that being labeled in a certain way will prompt them to improve in that direction. In other words, we treat adults as is the current fashion of treating children, that is, condescendingly. Since I'm not convinced that this is a good idea even where children are concerned, I am not surprised that it doesn't work very well with adults either.

That said, Miller does mention a few studies showing that virtue labeling has an effect (most of them, interestingly, carried out on children). For instance, back in 1975, researchers divided a group of fifth graders into three experimental treatments: some they labeled "tidy," some were asked to be tidy, and some served as controls and were given neither instructions nor labels.[8] Only children in the first treatment displayed tidier behavior. The problem is that there are very few such studies, and they are often about nonmoral traits, such as tidiness or competitiveness. Also, even when virtue labeling seems to work, we have no evidence that it does so in the long run. And there is a more subtle problem: Are people's characters actually improving, or are they simply responding to the labeling because they will feel ashamed if they don't live up to it? The difference is important because character is about motivations, and shame or embarrassment are not morally salient, as instrumentally effective as they may be. And one more thing: It should be disturbing if it turned out that we can get people to improve their behavior only by lying to them, which is what labeling irrespective of merit ends up doing.

The last strategy that turns out to be problematic is **nudging**. You've probably heard of this, as a number of governments and private companies have increasingly employed it in the last several years on the advice of some behavioral economists. If you are a man, you have likely encountered the most famous example of nudging: the fly in the urinal. Turns out that most men are, shall we say, absentminded when they urinate in a public facility, but they become far less messy if they are given a target to "hit" in the form of the image of a fly strategically located inside the urinal. Yes, people are strange. There are a number of other examples, from incentives to enroll in retirement plans to organ donations. A common strategy in nudging is to switch the default condition: Rather than waiting for someone to actively enroll in a given program, say, people are enrolled automatically unless they ask to opt out. This "libertarian paternalism" (an oxymoron?) takes advantage of the irrationality of aspects of human psychology but of course can be prone to nefarious use, depending on the motivations of the government agency or private company. We also have no evidence that nudging works in the long run, particularly, again, when it comes to morally salient behavior.

What, then, does work—empirically speaking—to improve our characters? Three strategies: the use of moral role models, conscious selecting of situations, and "getting the word out" (with ourselves). One reason this is fascinating and crucial to our discussion is that these three strategies have long been part and parcel of the *philosophical* approach to improving one's character. This parallel between research in modern psychology and ancient philosophy is perhaps most clear when we compare the three effective strategies to what the Stoics—the most pragmatically oriented of the Greco-Roman philosophers inspired by Socrates—recommended we do.

Let's begin with the notion of **adopting role models** after whom to pattern one's behavior. This seems to be an effective way to improve our character, and of course the motivation here (unlike that described above) is the right one: We want to become better people. Role models can be people we know (your grandfather, for instance), people we know of (Nelson Mandela), or even fictional entities (Spider-Man, everyone's favorite neighborhood superhero). The Stoics explicitly advised the use of role models. Here is the early-second-century Stoic philosopher Epictetus: "When you are about to meet someone, especially someone who seems to be distinguished, put to yourself the question, 'What would Socrates or Zeno have done in these circumstances?' and you will not be at a loss as to how to deal with the occasion."[9]

And here is the first-century Stoic writer Seneca: "Choose therefore a Cato; or, if Cato seems too severe a model, choose some Laelius, a gentler spirit. Choose a master whose life, conversation, and soul-expressing face have satisfied you; picture him always to yourself as your protector or your pattern. For we must indeed have someone according to whom we may regulate our characters; you can never straighten that which is crooked unless you use a ruler."[10]

There are good studies showing the efficacy of role models. One of my favorites concerns blood donations. Researchers have discovered that when a role model signed up for a donation, eighteen out of twenty other people signed up as well. Without a role model, the number of people who signed up to donate was zero.[11]

The second strategy that works well is one based on the idea of **purposely seeking out situations** that inspire us to do well while actively avoiding those that may go against our ethics. Miller's example is that of a flirtatious colleague who invites you to a secluded dinner. Just don't go. Instead, make sure never to see him without other people around, thus diminishing the temptation to engage in an ethically questionable affair. Conversely, seeking out inspiring situations can be most straightforwardly done by associating ourselves with people whom we judge to have a better character than ours so that we can learn by following, and participating in, their example.

The Stoics were on target here as well, as they suggested precisely these two ways to implement the situational strategy, as we may call it. For instance, "Just as he who tries to be rid of an old love must avoid every reminder of the person once held dear (for nothing grows again so easily as love), similarly, he who would lay aside his desire for all the things which he used to crave so passionately, must turn away both eyes and ears from the objects which he has abandoned. The emotions soon return to the attack."[12] And "Avoid fraternizing with non-philosophers. If you must, though, be careful not to sink to their level; because, you know, if a companion is dirty, his friends cannot help but get a little dirty too, no matter how clean they started out."[13]

"Non-philosophers" here, again, means not people who don't have a PhD in philosophy but people who don't try their best to follow a philosophical life, that is, a life of virtue. The implication of this quotation is that we should actively seek "philosophers," meaning virtuous people, as friends. If it sounds hopelessly snobbish, think of it simply as the advice your mom probably gave you when you were a kid: Beware of the company you keep.

Modern economists refer to this notion of seeking positive situations and avoiding negative ones as "precommitment strategies," and there is good evidence that they work. The more general notion is to actively shape our behavior by way of modifying the environment in which we operate. And since we, not anonymous, external "nudging" agents, must do the work, we are doing something not only because it is efficacious but also for the right reason—to cultivate our own character.

The last strategy that has good empirical backing is that of **getting the word out with ourselves**, so to speak. It really means getting to know who we are and what makes us tick. This is a question of mindfulness in the sense of paying attention to what we do and how we respond to situations, again with the goal of improving our character step by step. The empirical evidence is that we can even educate ourselves in order to counter nonconscious responses, such as the bystander effect. Recall that this is the situation where we tend not to act if someone is in distress in case there are other inactive people around us, likely because we don't want to misread the situation and embarrass ourselves. One study shows that people help in only 27 percent of the cases when the bystander effect is at play. However, if they are educated beforehand about the effect and pay attention to the situations they are in, the rate of helpful responses jumps to 67 percent.[14]

Here too the Stoics were way ahead of their time, as they practiced a type of mindfulness known as *prosochē*, which works pretty much along the lines just described: "Very little is needed for everything to be upset and ruined, only a slight lapse in reason. It's much easier for a mariner to wreck his ship than it is for him to keep it sailing safely; all he has to do is head a little more upwind and disaster is instantaneous. In fact, he does not have to do anything: a momentary loss of attention will produce the same result."[15]

Paying attention. Mindfulness. *Prosochē*. These clear parallels between one of the most explicitly Socratic philosophies of antiquity and modern research in social psychology brings me to the next question: What is the role of philosophy, if any, in shaping the character of potential leaders and political figures, and indeed of everyone else as well?

PHILOSOPHY: THE ART OF LIVING

As we have discussed, ever since Socrates, there have been two kinds of philosophers and two ways of doing philosophy. On the one hand, we have the likes of Descartes, Kant, Hegel, and almost everyone who is employed nowadays as a philosopher in academic departments. These are people who see philosophy as a type of theoretical inquiry into a variety of particular fields— from ethics to aesthetics, from logic to metaphysics. This tradition actually precedes Socrates, as it characterized those thinkers we refer to as "Presocratics," such as Thales of Miletus, Anaxagoras, Anaximenes, Parmenides, Heraclitus, and a number of others.

On the other hand, we have modern philosophers such as Nietzsche and Foucault, who follow in the steps of Socrates, the Stoics, the Epicureans, and several other Hellenistic schools in thinking of philosophy as a very practical matter, the art of living, if you will. Socrates was among the first in the Western tradition to turn away from a general interest in nature (metaphysics and natural philosophy, as practiced by most of the Presocratics) and toward human affairs, with a particular focus on ethics and politics. As modern scholar John Sellars puts it in his aptly titled *The Art of Living*, "For him, philosophy conceived as an art aspires to excellence and wisdom, and thus Socrates understands 'philosophy' in its etymological sense [i.e., love of wisdom]....A number of the Stoics including Epictetus appear to have understood the idea of an art of living as Socrates did."[16]

Philosophy conceived as the art of living has as its subject of concern one's "soul" (or character, in modern terms) and as its goal the betterment of this soul/character. The product of the practice is excellence, or wisdom in the broad sense of the term.

That is why we have been exploring how philosophers in the Socratic vein, beginning with Socrates himself, have attempted to influence the course of society for the better, either by teaching rulers, statesmen, and politicians or by taking on those roles themselves.

Broadly speaking, there is no reason why the two strands of philosophy should be mutually exclusive. One can be interested in, say, metaphysics and also strive to be a good person. Indeed, for the Stoics, not only was there no fundamental distinction between theoretical knowledge and practical wisdom but the latter required a certain amount of the former. This is clear in the commentary on the Stoics by Diogenes Laertius, who summarizes the three branches of philosophy according to Stoicism:

> [The Stoics] say that philosophical doctrine has three parts: the physical, the ethical, and the logical.... They compare philosophy to an animal, likening logic to the bones and sinews, ethics to the fleshier parts, and physics to the soul. Or again, they liken it to an egg: the outer parts are logic, the next parts are ethics, and the inmost parts are physics; or to a fertile field, of which logic is the surrounding fence, ethics the fruit, and physics the land or the trees. Or to a city that is well fortified and governed according to reason.[17]

The study of "physics" (i.e., metaphysics and natural philosophy) and "logic" (i.e., anything to do with good reasoning) is clearly theoretical. But it is necessary to develop one's "ethics" (i.e., one's life conduct). Why? Because if you go through life without a decent grasp of reality, that is, of how the world works, you are likely to make mistakes—possibly fatal ones. Refusing a vaccine in the middle of a pandemic, for instance, because you don't truly understand how viruses and pandemics work. But even if you do have a sufficient grasp of factual matters, you also need to reason correctly about them; otherwise, again, you will make mistakes. Incorrectly guessing the probability of being exposed to a virus, for instance, if you don't wear protective gear or maintain social distancing. Both factual understanding and sound reasoning, therefore, are essential components of an ethical life, meaning a life well lived.

Despite the importance of theory, a good philosophical life is largely a matter of practice. This primacy of practice over theory is particularly evident in Nietzsche, who argued that we should examine a philosopher's life rather than what he or she said or wrote. The ancients too suggested that studying philosophers' biographies is one of the best tools available to learn the art of living. This is why Zeno of Citium—the founder of Stoicism— began a momentous turn in his life by listening to Xenophon's *Memorabilia*, a biography of Socrates: "[Zeno] became a student of Crates under the following circumstances. Transporting a cargo of purple dye from Phoenicia to the Piraeus, he was shipwrecked. On reaching Athens (he was then a man of thirty), he sat down in a bookseller's shop. The bookseller was reading aloud the second book of Xenophon's *Memorabilia*, and Zeno was so pleased that he asked where such men could be found. At that very moment, fortunately, Crates happened to be walking past. Pointing him out, the bookseller said, 'Follow him.'"[18]

As usual, it all goes back to Socrates. In the Platonic dialogue known as the *Gorgias*, we find Socrates arguing that mastering principles is necessary but not sufficient; one also needs some kind of practical training. In other words, philosophy conceived as the art of living involves both theory and practice, and it is the latter that turns those who make progress into good human beings. Epictetus, who patterned his own behavior on that of Socrates, says so explicitly: "The philosophers first exercise us in theory, where there is less difficulty, and then after that lead us to the more difficult matters; for in theory there is nothing which holds us back from following what we are taught, but in the affairs of life there are many things which draw us away."[19]

Epictetus is not implying that theory is secondary. On the contrary, it is the guide to practice, and one simply can't practice without first having a minimum theoretical background. This connection between theory and practice may be clearly understood by way of an analogy with athletics that was in fact often used by both Socrates and the Stoics. If you decide to go to the gym to improve your aerobic capacity and muscle tone, you will need to know how to properly use the various machines, weights, and so on (theory), but you also must do it regularly and for long periods of time (practice), or you won't see the results. Needless to say, just as Epictetus states, the practice is harder than the theory.

The person aspiring to the philosophical life engages in spiritual exercises rather than physical exercises. Here the "spiritual" attribute comes from the modern French scholar Pierre Hadot. Hadot, in turn, gets it from the founder of the Jesuits, Ignatius of Loyola. This is Loyola's definition: "The term 'spiritual exercises' denotes every way of examining one's conscience, of meditating, contemplating, praying vocally and mentally, and other spiritual activities, as will be said later. For just as strolling, walking, and running are exercises for the body, so 'spiritual exercises' is the name given to every way of preparing and disposing one's soul to rid herself of all disordered attachments, so that once rid of them one might seek and find the divine will in regard to the disposition of one's life for the good of the soul."[20]

Compare this with what the Stoic Musonius Rufus, Epictetus's teacher, said fifteen centuries before Loyola:

> Training which is peculiar to the soul consists first of all in
> seeing that the proofs pertaining to apparent goods as not being
> real goods are always ready at hand and likewise those pertain-
> ing to apparent evils as not being real evils, and in learning
> to recognize the things which are truly good and in becoming
> accustomed to distinguish them from what are not truly good.
> In the next place it consists of practice in not avoiding any of
> the things which only seem evil, and in not pursuing any of
> the things which only seem good; in shunning by every means
> those which are truly evil and in pursuing by every means those
> which are truly good.[21]

Musonius is deploying a concept very much along the lines of
Loyola, though he is being more specific as to what, exactly, the
spiritual exercises in question—according to Stoic doctrine—
consist of. In order to avoid an easy misunderstanding, let me
stress that "spiritual," in this context, does not imply any particular conception about the soul. Certainly Loyola held the
Christian view in this matter, and Musonius held the materialist
understanding of the soul that accompanied Stoic pantheism.
We moderns can simply speak of mental exercises without loss
of meaning.

But how do we engage in spiritual (or mental) philosophical exercises? Galen, Marcus Aurelius's personal physician,
explains, "All we must do is keep the doctrine regarding in-
satiability and self-sufficiency constantly at hand, and commit
ourselves to the daily exercise of the particular actions which
follow from these doctrines."[22]

This, it turns out, translates into two themes emerging from the ancient literature on spiritual exercises: habituation and digestion. Let's start by considering habituation. For Musonius Rufus, spiritual exercises consist of training ourselves to more effectively distinguish between real and apparent goods. His student Epictetus elaborates, "At everything that happens to you remember to turn to yourself and find what capacity you have to deal with it. If you see a beautiful boy or girl, you will find self-control as the capacity to deal with it; if hard labor is imposed on you, you will find endurance; if abuse, you will find patience. And when you make a habit of this, the impressions will not carry you away."[23]

Marcus Aurelius, who was strongly influenced by Epictetus, returns often to the theme of habituation: "As are your repeated imaginations so will your mind be, for the soul is dyed by its imaginations. Dye it, then, in a succession of imaginations like these."[24]

Habituation gradually alters character and allows us to translate theory into practice.

What about "digestion"? Epictetus uses the term explicitly, warning his students that unless they have properly digested Stoic doctrines, they won't be able to practice them but will simply "vomit" them to others.[25] All talk and no action, so to speak. Seneca too uses the metaphor of digestion in one of his letters to his friend Lucilius: "Be careful lest this reading of many authors and books of every sort may tend to make you discursive and unsteady. You must linger among a limited number of master-thinkers and digest their works.... For food does no good and is not assimilated into the body if it leaves the stomach as soon as it is eaten, and nothing hinders a cure so much as frequent change of medicine.... Each day...after you have run over many thoughts, select one to be thoroughly digested that day."[26]

To understand the practice a bit more clearly, let's consider the typical ancient curriculum of practical philosophy. John Sellars, in his *The Art of Living*, provides a nice summary of the three types of texts the ancients used to train themselves:

Literature concerned with action: biographies and anecdotal material, so that one can use the life of good philosophers as a pattern for one's own.

Literature concerned with arguments and doctrines: theoretical treatises and commentaries, so that one can understand why it is better to live a certain kind of life rather than another one.

Literature concerned with practical ("spiritual") exercises: either guides to practice or examples of practice, so that one can go to the spiritual gym on a regular basis.

The notion was to first acquaint students with the life of good role models through reading biographies so that they would obtain an intuitive idea of what they should aspire to (one could also study *bad* role models to grasp what one should avoid). The second step was the study of theoretical treatises for a more in-depth understanding of the principles behind one's chosen philosophy. Finally, students would turn to practical exercises to implement the theory and to, hopefully, mold their lives along the lines of the exemplars with whom they started.

Whether we are a politician with the opportunity to guide an entire people in a better direction or a private individual influencing only our loved ones and friends does not matter. It seems to me that all of us in the modern era may have reason to desire a return to a conception of philosophy understood—and practiced—as the art of living. Indeed, that conception has never actually disappeared. While we tend to think of people such as Socrates and Epictetus, semilost in the mists of time, philosophy was practiced throughout the Middles Ages (e.g., Peter Abelard, John of Salisbury) and the Renaissance (Petrarch's *On the Remedies of Both Kinds of Fortune*, Justus Lipsius and his Neostoicism). The modern era has seen advocates of practiced philosophy as well. I've already mentioned Nietzsche and Foucault. Currently, we are seeing a resurgence of interest in Stoicism, Epicureanism, Buddhism, Confucianism, and Daoism, among other lived philosophical traditions. Sellars reminds us that it is highly misleading to characterize practical philosophy as "ancient" and to think of theoretical philosophical inquiry (metaphysics, natural philosophy) as modern. As we have seen, they have both existed since the Presocratics (not to mention in Indian and Chinese philosophy): two parallel, non–mutually exclusive, and in fact reciprocally reinforcing ways to think about, and do, philosophy.

The very theme of this book—gaining an understanding of the ancient connections between philosophy and politics and how we can use this understanding to better ourselves in the modern era—suggests a call to examination of our own character and from there to expand outward to improve our communities and our society. In that spirit, I'd like to conclude by suggesting a syllabus for the self-study of practical philosophy along the lines sketched above, largely based on the most pragmatically oriented of ancient Western philosophies: Stoicism.

The way to take full advantage of the syllabus is to do the readings in the proposed sequence, write about them in a dedicated philosophical journal in which you track your progress, and—if possible—discuss them with other practitioners.[27] I have organized the syllabus in modules without specifying a particular pace per module because people will have different amounts of time to devote to this study. However, as Seneca says, don't slack off: "Are you not ashamed to reserve for yourself only the remnant of life, and to set apart for wisdom only that time which cannot be devoted to any business?"[28]

THE ART OF LIVING—A POSSIBLE COURSE OF SELF-STUDY

Here is how to use this syllabus. Proceed in sequence from one module to the next, at whatever pace is comfortable for you, so long as your readings are consistent and not just occasional. Take notes in a separate diary about your thoughts concerning each entry. Feel free to switch back and forth between the biographical, theoretical, and practical modules without skipping too far ahead (e.g., alternate Modules I, II, and III but finish this group before you move to IV, V, and VI).

Start a philosophical journal of ethical self-improvement. In the journal, reflect not just on the content of your readings but also on what it means to you, and especially on how it should affect your behavior in everyday life as well as your overall view of your life trajectory. If possible, discuss your progress with friends or fellow practitioners of the art of living.

If you are so inclined, send the syllabus to an aspiring or elected politician. Or at least, to friends and family.

Module I—Biographical role models, 1

Diogenes Laertius, *The Lives of the Eminent Philosophers*. Diogenes Laertius is arguably our most comprehensive source on the lives and thought of the preeminent ancient philosophers in the Western tradition. Remember, these are intended to be moral biographies. Diogenes's accounts are valuable because of how the lives he writes about may inspire us. He is not always careful with the biographical details, which is not atypical of ancient writers who did not necessarily share our contemporary notion of factual accuracy. Sometimes you may find that Diogenes even gets some philosophical principles wrong. But the point is to open one of his chapters and read for inspiration and direction. How did others live? What choices did they make? How do the questions asked in these texts relate to questions we face in our modern lives?

I especially recommend the sections on Socrates, Aristippus, Plato, Aristotle, Diogenes of Sinope, Hipparchia, Zeno of Citium, Cleanthes, Heraclitus, Zeno of Elea, and Epicurus.

Module II—Theory, 1

Epictetus, *Discourses*. This is a compilation of short speeches by the Stoic philosopher Epictetus as well as conversations he had with his students. It was put together by Arrian of Nicomedia, one of Epictetus's most prominent students, and it gives us an excellent feel for both Stoic philosophy and Epictetus's dynamic personality. Unfortunately, only four of the original eight "books" survive, but the wealth of material and the span of topics is breathtaking. It helps that each section comes with a descriptive title, which can guide the reader interested in specific applications.

Here are some of my favorites: "Of the things which are under our control and not under our control" (I.1), "Of the use of equivocal premises, hypothetical arguments and the like" (I.7), "Of family affection" (I.11), "That the art of reasoning is indispensable" (I.17), "That we ought not to be angry with the erring" (I.18), "How ought we to bear ourselves toward tyrants?" (I.19), "Of our preconceptions" (I.22), "In answer to Epicurus" (I.23), "How should we struggle against difficulties?" (I.24), "On tranquillity" (II.2), "To the man who had once been caught in adultery" (II.4), "What is the true nature of the good?" (II.8), "What is the beginning of philosophy?" (II.11), "Of anxiety" (II.13), "Of friendship" (II.22), "How is logic necessary?" (II.25), "Of personal adornment" (III.1), "How ought we to bear our illness?" (III.10), "Of training" (III.12), "That one should enter cautiously into social intercourse" (III.16), "On the calling of a Cynic" (III.22), "To those who read and discuss for the purpose of display" (III.23), "That we ought not to yearn for the things that are not under our control" (III.24), "To those who fear want" (III.26), "Of freedom" (IV.1), "Of social intercourse" (IV.2), "What things should be exchanged for what things?" (IV.3), "Against the contentious and brutal" (IV.5), "Of freedom from fear" (IV.7), "Of cleanliness" (IV.11), and "Of attention" (IV.12).

Module III—Practice, 1

Marcus Aurelius, *Meditations.* This famous book was actually not meant for publication, as it was the emperor's personal philosophical diary. Philosophical journaling is a fundamental technique for Stoic practice, the efficacy of which has been confirmed by modern cognitive behavioral therapy. You could use Marcus's words as both an inspiration and a broad template. You will see that he writes in the second person, as if he were addressing a friend. This approach, according to contemporary psychologists, has the advantage of helping to put some emotional distance between you and the life episodes you are describing so that an analytical approach comes more easily. Note that the *Meditations* don't have any particular structure, as you would expect in a diary. They are also somewhat repetitive and "preachy," again as you would expect given that this was the personal journal of someone who was chiding himself in order to make progress. The glaring exception is "book" I, which is really an extended exercise in gratitude, where Marcus lists the major people who influenced him in his life and elaborates on what they taught him. Gratitude exercises are another standard tool in the Stoic toolbox and are also practiced within other philosophical traditions.

Module IV—Biographical role models, 2

Xenophon, *Memorabilia*. Much of what we know about Socrates's philosophy comes from Plato. But Xenophon's *Memorabilia* tells us a lot more about Socrates the man. In reading it, we get a vivid sense of what the philosopher's day must have been like, how he interacted with other people, and what his concerns were. We also find an interesting defense of Socrates by one of his close friends. This is the book that, in a way, got Stoicism started, as it was the *Memorabilia* that turned Zeno of Citium, the founder of the Stoa, to philosophy.

Module V—Theory, 2

Seneca, *On Anger*. Although this book may appear to be narrowly focused, as its main topic is a particular instance of what the Stoics referred to as unhealthy emotions, that is, emotions that go against reason, it is one of the most important surviving

Stoic texts. By discussing anger, Seneca gives us a broad over-view of how the Stoics treated emotions in general, contrast-ing the unhealthy ones (anger, fear, hatred, and so on) with the healthy ones (love, joy, a sense of justice, and so forth). It also includes a sophisticated description of the nature and stages of anger as well as practical advice on anger management that is still pretty much what is recommended by the American Psy-chological Association. And it's beautifully written.

Module VI—Practice, 2

Epictetus, *Enchiridion*, the short manual for a good life. These fifty-three short sections were compiled by Arrian of Nicome-dia, Epictetus's student, to summarize the *Discourses* and there-fore the fundamentals of Epictetus's philosophy. They provide clear guidance for actual behavior following Stoic precepts, and the book is supposed to be used as a vade mecum (carry-with-you), to be consulted when needed.

I published an update of the *Enchiridion* for the twenty-first century titled *A Field Guide to a Happy Life: 53 Brief Lessons for Living*. You may want to add it to your module and draw cross-comparisons with Epictetus's original.

Module VII—Biographical role models, 3

Plutarch, *Parallel Lives*. This classic is not just about philos-ophers, and certainly not specifically about Stoicism. Indeed, Plutarch was a prominent critic of the Stoics. But his parallel portraits of famous people from antiquity are meant to be the quintessential guide to spotting good and bad moral behavior. To make the task easier, Plutarch often even directly compares the members of each pair to each other after having summarized their individual lives.

Particularly noteworthy are Solon and Publicola, Themistocles and Camillus, Pericles and Fabius Maximus, Alcibiades and Coriolanus, Lysander and Sulla, Nicias and Crassus, Agesilaus and Pompey, Alexander and Caesar, Phocion and Cato the Younger, Demosthenes and Cicero, and Dion and Brutus.

Module VIII—Theory, 3

Seneca, *Letters to Lucilius.* These 124 letters from Seneca to his friend Lucilius are described by classicist Liz Gloyn as an informal curriculum in Stoic philosophy. Seneca cyclically revisits a number of themes, becoming increasingly in-depth in their treatment.

Some of my favorites are "On saving time" (1), "On true and false friendship" (3), "On the terrors of death" (4), "On crowds" (7), "On old age" (12), "On philosophy and riches" (17), "On festivals and fasting" (18), "On practicing what you preach" (20), "On travel as a cure for discontent" (28), "On the value of retirement" (36), "On master and slave" (47), "On the shortness of life" (49), "On choosing our teachers" (52), "On asthma and death" (54), "On quiet and study" (56), "On pleasure and joy" (59), "On grief for lost friends" (63), "On ill-health and endurance of suffering" (67), "On the proper time to slip the cable" (70), "On business as the enemy of philosophy" (72), "On the rewards of scientific discovery" (79), "On benefits" (81), "On some vain syllogisms" (85), "On the happy life" (92), "On the quality, as contrasted with the length, of life" (93), "On the usefulness of basic principles" (95), "On the fickleness of fortune" (98), "On the futility of planning ahead" (101), "On true and false riches" (110), "On the vanity of mental gymnastics" (111), "On style as a mirror of character" (114), "On self-control" (116), "On the conflict between pleasure and virtue" (123), and "On the true good as attained by reason" (124).

Module IX—Practice, 3

At the cost of being immodest, here I put my own *Handbook for New Stoics*, coauthored with my friend Greg Lopez. It is a rather unique book among modern offerings because it is highly focused on philosophical practice. It contains fifty-two exercises, grouped according to the three standard disciplines outlined by Epictetus: desire and aversion (about how to reorganize our priorities in life), action (how to act in the world, particularly with regard to other people), and assent (how to sharpen our faculty of judgment). Each exercise is culled from the ancient Stoic literature and updated with the latest from psychology and cognitive science.

If we take seriously the goal of ethical self-improvement, then we need to study and practice, and the above syllabus is meant as a step-by-step aid in doing so. It is no different than working on our bodily health, say, by going to the gym or deciding to eat more wholesome food. In both cases, we need a bit of theory (e.g., knowledge of the most appropriate exercise routines or the sorts of foodstuffs that are good or bad for us) and then a lot of practice, day after day. Now if we could only convince our wannabe political leaders to engage in this sort of regime...

ACKNOWLEDGMENTS

Writing a book is a solitary, difficult, yet wonderful experience, but it is possible only because of the help and influence of many people. I wish to thank my wife, Jennifer, for her encouragement and for carefully reading and commenting on a previous draft of this book. Many thanks also to two people who have become pivotal in my career as an author: my agent, Tisse Takagi, and my editor, TJ Kelleher. The manuscript has greatly benefited from the careful work of my copy editor, Connie Oehring. Finally, I would not have gotten to the point of being able to even think the thoughts expressed in this book if not for the example and influence of several of my colleagues, beginning with Rob Colter, Christian Miller, Don Robertson, and John Sellars, among many others.

SUGGESTED READINGS

1—CAN VIRTUE BE TAUGHT?

Aristotle, *Nicomachean Ethics*, translated by R. C. Bartlett and S. D. Collins, University of Chicago Press, 2012.

Cicero, *On Duties*, ed. by E. M. Atkins, translated by M. T. Griffin, Cambridge University Press, 1991.

Massimo Pigliucci, *How to Be a Stoic: Using Ancient Philosophy to Live a Modern Life*, Basic Books, 2017.

Plato, *Protagoras and Meno*, translated by A. Beresford, Penguin Classics, 2006.

John Sellars, *Hellenistic Philosophy*, Oxford University Press, 2018.

Frans de Waal et al., *Primates and Philosophers: How Morality Evolved*, Princeton University Press, 2006.

Catherine Wilson, *How to Be an Epicurean: The Ancient Art of Living Well*, Basic Books, 2019.

2—ALAS, ALCIBIADES, WHAT A CONDITION YOU SUFFER FROM!

John M. Cooper and D. S. Hutchinson (eds.), *Plato: Complete Works*, Hackett, 1997.

Pierre Destrée and Zina Giannopoulou (eds.), *Plato's Symposium: A Critical Guide*, Cambridge University Press, 2019.

Herodotus, *The Histories*, translated by Robin Waterfield, Oxford University Press, 2008.

David Johnson, *Socrates and Alcibiades: Four Texts: Plato's Alcibiades I & II, Symposium (212c–223a), Aeschines' Alcibiades*, Focus, 2002.
Xenophon, *Apologia*, Project Gutenberg, online at https://www .gutenberg.org/files/1171/1171-h/1171-h.htm.

3—A STRONG-MINDED CHILD

Steven Forde, *The Ambition to Rule: Alcibiades and the Politics of Imperialism in Thucydides*, Cornell University Press, 1989.
Plutarch, *Complete Works*, Delphi Classics, 2013.
David Stuttard, *Nemesis: Alcibiades and the Fall of Athens*, Harvard University Press, 2018.

4—THE GADFLY OF ATHENS

Aristophanes, *Complete Plays*, translated by B. B. Rogers, R. H. Webb, Moses Hadas, and Jack Lindsay, Bantam Classics, 1984.
Armand D'Angour, *Socrates in Love: The Making of a Philosopher*, Bloomsbury, 2019.
Harry G. Frankfurt, *On Bullshit*, Princeton University Press, 2005.
Paul Johnson, *Socrates: A Man for Our Times*, Viking, 2011.
Thomas L. Pangle, *The Socratic Way of Life: Xenophon's "Memorabilia,"* University of Chicago Press, 2020.
Plato, *Complete Works*, edited by John M. Cooper and D. S. Hutchinson, Hackett Publishing, 1997.

5—TEACHING VIRTUE TO POLITICIANS

Francis Caldwell Holland, *The Stoic*, online at https://archive.org /details/seneca__00holluoft.
Andrey Kortunov, "Aristotle and Alexander: two perspectives on globalization," *Modern Diplomacy*, January 1, 2021, online at https:// moderndiplomacy.eu/2021/01/01/aristotle-and-alexander-two -perspectives-on-globalization/.
Nick Romeo, "When philosopher met king: on Plato's Italian voyages," *Aeon*, December 21, 2020, online at https://aeon.co/essays /when-philosopher-met-king-on-platos-italian-voyages.
James Romm, *Dying Every Day: Seneca at the Court of Nero*, Vintage, 2014.

Michael Tierney, "Aristotle and Alexander the Great," *Studies* 31(122):221–228, June 1942.

Emily Wilson, *The Greatest Empire: A Life of Seneca*, Oxford University Press, 2018.

6—PHILOSOPHER-KINGS, ANYONE?

Anthony R. Birley, *Marcus Aurelius: A Biography*, Routledge, 2000.

Olivia Goldhill, "Ethicists are no more ethical than the rest of us, study finds," *Quartz*, March 27, 2019, online at https://qz.com/1582149/ethicists-are-no-more-ethical-than-the-rest-of-us-study-finds/.

Rob Goodman and Jimmy Soni, *Rome's Last Citizen: The Life and Legacy of Cato, Mortal Enemy of Caesar*, St. Martin's Griffin, 2014.

Pierre Hadot, *Philosophy as a Way of Life. Spiritual Exercises from Socrates to Foucault*, Blackwell, 1995.

Pierre Hadot, *The Inner Citadel: The Meditations of Marcus Aurelius*, Harvard University Press, 2001.

Julian, *Complete Works*, translated by Wilmer C. Wright, Delphi Classics, 2017.

Frank McLynn, *Marcus Aurelius: A Life*, Da Capo Press, 2010.

Gore Vidal, *Julian: A Novel*, Vintage, reprint 2018.

Paul Barron Watson, *Marcus Aurelius Antoninus*, Palala Press, (1884) 2016.

7—PHILOSOPHY AND POLITICS

Aristotle, *Politics*, translated by R. F. Stalley and Ernest Barker, Oxford University Press, 2009.

John Bew, *Realpolitik: A History*, Oxford University Press, 2018.

Thomas Hobbes, *Leviathan*, Penguin Classics, 2017.

Immanuel Kant, *To Perpetual Peace: A Philosophical Sketch*, translated by Ted Humphrey, Hackett Publishing, 2003.

John Locke, *Two Treatises of Government*, Cambridge University Press, 1988.

Niccolò Machiavelli, *The Prince*, translated by Tim Parks, Penguin, 2015.

Plato, *Republic*, translated by G. M. A. Grube, revised by C. D. C. Reeve, Hackett Publishing, 1992.

Sun Tzu, *The Art of War*, translated by Michael Nylan, W. W. Norton & Company, 2020.

8—IT'S ALL ABOUT CHARACTER

Marcus Aurelius, *Meditations: The Annotated Edition*, translated by Robin Waterfield, Basic Books, 2021.

Katherine Dahlsgaard, Christopher Peterson, and Martin E. P. Seligman, "Shared Virtue: The Convergence of Valued Human Strengths Across Culture and History," *Review of General Psychology* 9(3):203–213, 2005.

Epictetus, *Discourses, Fragments, Handbook*, translated by Robin Hard, Oxford University Press, 2014.

Diogenes Laertius, *Lives of the Eminent Philosophers*, translated by Pamela Mensch, Oxford University Press, 2018.

Christian Miller, *The Character Gap: How Good Are We?*, Oxford University Press, 2017.

Christian Miller, "Empirical Approaches to Moral Character," *Stanford Encyclopedia of Philosophy*, 2016, online at https://plato.stanford.edu/entries/moral-character-empirical/.

Massimo Pigliucci, *A Field Guide to a Happy Life: 53 Brief Lessons for Living*, Basic Books, 2020.

Massimo Pigliucci and Gregory Lopez, *A Handbook for New Stoics—How to Thrive in a World Out of Your Control: 52 Week-by-Week Lessons*, The Experiment, 2019.

Musonius Rufus, *Lectures and Sayings*, translated by Cynthia King, CreateSpace, 2011.

John Sellars, *The Art of Living: The Stoics on the Nature and Function of Philosophy*, Bristol Classical Press, 2009.

Seneca, *Anger, Mercy, Revenge*, translated by Robert A. Kaster and Martha C. Nussbaum, University of Chicago Press, 2010.

Seneca, *Letters on Ethics*, translated by Margaret Graver and A. A. Long, University of Chicago Press, 2015.

Seneca, *Hardship and Happiness*, translated by Elaine Fantham, Harry M. Hine, James Ker, and Gareth D. Williams, University of Chicago Press, 2014.

NOTES

1—CAN VIRTUE BE TAUGHT?

1. Plato, *Republic*, IV, 426–435.

2. Cicero, *On Duties*, I, V, and following.

3. K. Dahlsgaard, C. Peterson, and M. E. P. Seligman, "Shared virtue: the convergence of valued human strengths across culture and history," *Review of General Psychology* 9(3):203–213, 2005.

4. Catherine Wilson, *How to Be an Epicurean: The Ancient Art of Living Well*, Basic Books, 2019.

5. Massimo Pigliucci, *How to Be a Stoic: Using Ancient Philosophy to Live a Modern Life*, Basic Books, 2017.

6. Frans de Waal et al., *Primates and Philosophers: How Morality Evolved*, Princeton University Press, 2006.

7. Plato, *Meno*, 70a.

8. Plato, *Protagoras*, 319b.

9. *Protagoras*, 319e.

10. *Protagoras*, 327b–d.

11. *Meno*, 84c.

12. H. M. Curtler, "Can virtue be taught?," *Humanitas* 7(1), 1994.

13. Aristotle, *Nicomachean Ethics*, 1103a.14–19.

14. R. R. McCrae and P. T. Costa, "The stability of personality: observations and evaluations," *Current Directions in Psychological Science* 3(6):173–175, 1994.

15. J. Pujol, P. Vendrell, C. Junqué, J. L. Martí-Vilalta, and A. Capdevila, "When does human brain development end? Evidence of corpus

callosum growth up to adulthood," *Annals of Neurology* 34(1):71–75, 1993.

16. "Can virtue be taught?," 48–49.

17. Epictetus, *Discourses*, I.5.4.

2—ALAS, ALCIBIADES, WHAT A CONDITION YOU SUFFER FROM!

1. Plato, *Alcibiades I*, 17.
2. Xenophon, *Apologia*, 14.
3. Plato, *Alcibiades I*, 26.
4. Herodotus, *Histories*, 7.114.
5. Plato, *Alcibiades I*, 57.
6. Plato, *Alcibiades II*, 150d.
7. Thomas Aquinas, *Summa Theologiae*, I–II, 26, 4.
8. Plato, *Symposium*, 215d.
9. *Symposium*, 216c.
10. *Symposium*, 216e.
11. *Symposium*, 219.

3—A STRONG-MINDED CHILD

1. Plutarch, *Lives—Alcibiades*, 11.
2. *Alcibiades*, 12.2.
3. *Alcibiades*, 16.3.
4. *Alcibiades*, 7.2.
5. Plato, *Symposium*, 283–284.
6. Diogenes Laertius, *Lives of the Eminent Philosophers*, translated by Pamela Mensch, Oxford University Press, 2018, II.22.
7. Thucydides, *History of the Peloponnesian War*, VI.6.
8. *History of the Peloponnesian War*, VI.16.
9. *Alcibiades*, 17.4.
10. *Alcibiades*, 22.2.
11. *Alcibiades*.
12. *History of the Peloponnesian War*, VI.92.
13. *History of the Peloponnesian War*, VIII.46.
14. *History of the Peloponnesian War*, VIII.82.
15. Xenophon, *Hellenica*, I.4.20.

16. *Alcibiades*, 39.1.

17. *Alcibiades*, 39.5.

18. *History of the Peloponnesian War*, V.43.

19. *History of the Peloponnesian War*, VI.15.

20. *History of the Peloponnesian War*, VI.16.

21. Plutarch, *Lives—Alexander the Great*, 1.1–3.

22. Plutarch, *Lives—Comparison of Alcibiades and Coriolanus*, 1.4.

23. *Comparison of Alcibiades and Coriolanus*, 2.3.

24. *Comparison of Alcibiades and Coriolanus*, 4.6.

4—THE GADFLY OF ATHENS

1. Harry G. Frankfurt, *On Bullshit*, Princeton University Press, 2005.

2. Xenophon, *Memorabilia*, II.2.1.

3. *Memorabilia*, II.2.3.

4. *Memorabilia*, II.2.5.

5. *Memorabilia*, II.2.8.

6. *Memorabilia*, II.2.9–10.

7. *Memorabilia*, II.2.14.

8. *Memorabilia*, III.6.3–4.

9. *Memorabilia*, III.6.8.

10. *Memorabilia*, III.6.11.

11. *Memorabilia*, III.6.15–16.

12. *Memorabilia*, III.7.1.

13. *Memorabilia*, III.7.4.

14. *Memorabilia*, III.7.9.

15. *Memorabilia*, IV.2.1.

16. *Memorabilia*, IV.2.2.

17. *Memorabilia*, IV.2.5.

18. *Memorabilia*, IV.2.6.

19. *Memorabilia*, IV.2.11–12.

20. *Memorabilia*, IV.2.19.

21. *Memorabilia*, IV.2.24.

22. *Memorabilia*, IV.2.26.

23. *Memorabilia*, IV.2.27.

24. *Memorabilia*, IV.2.31–32.

25. *Memorabilia*, IV.2.34–35.

26. *Memorabilia*, IV.2.40.
27. *Memorabilia*, I.1.1.
28. *Memorabilia*, I.1.2.
29. *Memorabilia*, I.1.4–5.
30. *Memorabilia*, I.1.10.
31. *Memorabilia*, I.1.11.
32. *Memorabilia*, I.1.16.
33. *Memorabilia*, I.1.18.
34. *Memorabilia*, I.2.1.
35. *Memorabilia*, I.2.8.
36. *Memorabilia*, I.2.24.
37. *Memorabilia*, I.2.27.
38. *Memorabilia*, I.3.1.
39. *Memorabilia*, I.3.5
40. *Memorabilia*, I.3.6,8.
41. *Memorabilia*, I.4.5–6.
42. *Memorabilia*, I.5.1.
43. *Memorabilia*, I.6.15.

5—TEACHING VIRTUE TO POLITICIANS

1. Plato, *Seventh Letter*, 327b.
2. Plato, *Republic*, VIII.
3. Plutarch, *Dion*, 5.3.
4. *Dion*, 7.4.
5. Plato, *Seventh Letter*, 330a.
6. Plutarch, *Life of Alexander*, 8.2.
7. *Life of Alexander*, 7.5.
8. *Life of Alexander*, 7.7.
9. Plutarch, *On the fortune or the virtue of Alexander*, 2.
10. *On the fortune or the virtue of Alexander*, 1.
11. *On the fortune or the virtue of Alexander*, 1.6.
12. Seneca, *Letters to Lucilius*, 13, 17.
13. In *The Complete Works of Seneca the Younger*, Delphi Classics, 2014.
14. Anna Lydia Motto, "Seneca on Trial: The Case of the Opulent Stoic," *Classic Journal* 61, 257, 1966.

15. Martha Nussbaum, *The Therapy of Desire: Theory and Practice in Hellenistic Ethics*, Princeton University Press, 1996.

16. Martha Nussbaum, *Cultivating Humanity: A Classical Defense of Reform in Liberal Education*, Harvard University Press, 1999.

17. Robert Wagoner, "Lucius Annaeus Seneca," *Internet Encyclopedia of Philosophy*, https://iep.utm.edu/seneca/.

18. *Letters to Lucilius*, 118, 8–9.

19. Seneca, *On Clemency*, 1.1.

20. *On Clemency*, 1.1.

21. *On Clemency*, 1.2.

22. *On Clemency*, 1.5.

23. *On Clemency*, 1.7.

24. *On Clemency*, 1.8.

25. *On Clemency*, 1.11.

26. *On Clemency*, 1.12.

27. *On Clemency*, 1.17.

28. *On Clemency*, 1.20.

29. *On Clemency*, 1.22.

30. *On Clemency*, 1.25.

31. *On Clemency*, 1.26.

32. *On Clemency*, 2.6.

6—PHILOSOPHER-KINGS, ANYONE?

1. Plato, *Phaedo*, 98c.

2. E. Schwitzgebel and J. Rust, "The moral behavior of ethics professors: Relationships among self-reported behavior, expressed normative attitude, and directly observed behavior," *Philosophical Psychology* 27(3), 2014.

3. Seneca, *Letters to Lucilius*, 71,11.

4. Plutarch, *Cato the Younger*, 2.

5. Rob Goodman and Jimmy Soni, *Rome's Last Citizen*, 19.

6. Lucan, *Pharsalia*, IX.738–746.

7. *Rome's Last Citizen*, 246.

8. Plutarch, *Cato the Younger*, 57.2.

9. *Cato the Younger*, 70.5–6.

10. *Cato the Younger*, 72.2.

11. *Rome's Last Citizen*, 280.

12. *Pharsalia*, I.128.

13. Dante, *Convivio*, 4.28.15.

14. Ron Chernow, *Washington: A Life*, Penguin, 2010, 75.

15. Alexander Pope, personal letter to John Caryll, April 30, 1713, in *The Works of Alexander Pope*, John Murray, 1871, vol. 6, 183.

16. Voltaire, *Letters on England*, Penguin, 1980, 18.

17. John Trenchard and Thomas Gordon, *Cato's Letters*, Liberty Fund, 1995, Letter 99.

18. Cassius Dio, *Roman History*, 72, 36.3.

19. Marcus Aurelius, *Meditations*, 1.7.

20. *Meditations*, 1.6.

21. *Meditations*, 1.7.

22. "The Sayings of Marcus," *Delphi Complete Works of Marcus Aurelius*, 2014, 19.

23. Pierre Hadot, *The Inner Citadel*, Harvard University Press, 2001, 18.

24. *Meditations*, 1.17.10.

25. *Meditations*, 5.5.1.

26. Cassius Dio, *Roman History*, 72, 34.4–5.

27. *The Inner Citadel*, 292.

28. *Meditations*, 1.14.1.

29. *Meditations*, 1.14.2.

30. Seneca, *Letters to Lucilius*, 47.10.

31. Dio Chrysostom, *On Slavery and Freedom*, 15.26.

32. Epictetus, Fragment 38.

33. Aristotle, *Politics*, 1.

34. Paul Barron Watson, *Marcus Aurelius Antoninus*, Palala Press, (1884) 2016, 105.

35. Bertrand Russell, *The History of Western Philosophy*, Simon & Schuster, 1945, 270.

36. C. R. Haines, *Introduction to Marcus Aurelius' Meditations*, Delphi Classics, 2014.

37. *Meditations*, 8.48.51.

38. Quoted in D. Robertson, "Did Marcus Aurelius persecute the Christians?," https://donaldrobertson.name/2017/01/13/did-marcus -aurelius-persecute-the-christians/.

39. C. R. Haines, *Marcus Aurelius*, Harvard University Press, 1916.

40. *Meditations*, 11.3.

41. Frank McLynn, *Marcus Aurelius: A Life*, Da Capo Press, 2010, 404.

42. *Meditations*, 9.12.

7—PHILOSOPHY AND POLITICS

1. E. Harmon-Jones (ed.), *Cognitive Dissonance: Reexamining a Pivotal Theory in Psychology*, American Psychological Association, 2019; E. Aronson, "Dissonance, hypocrisy, and the self-concept," in E. Harmon-Jones (ed.), *Cognitive Dissonance: Reexamining a Pivotal Theory in Psychology*, American Psychological Association, 141–157.

2. J. S. Mill, *Utilitarianism*, Parker, Son, and Bourn, 1863, chapter 2, available online at https://www.utilitarianism.com/mill1.htm.

3. "The Last Outpost," *Star Trek: The Next Generation*, episode I.5.

4. Niccolò Machiavelli, "States won by lucky circumstance and someone else's armed forces," *The Prince*, Penguin Classics, 2009, 7.

5. Quoted in Joshua Kaplan, "Political Theory: The Classic Texts and Their Continuing Relevance," *Modern Scholar*, 2005.

6. Introduction to *The Prince*.

7. Thomas Hobbes, *Leviathan*, XIII.9.

8. Epictetus, *Discourses*, I.9.1.

9. Marcus Aurelius, *Meditations*, VI.44.

10. Ludwig von Rochau, *Principles of Realpolitik Applied to the National State of Affairs of Germany*, K. Göpel, 1859.

11. *Meditations*, IX.29.

8—IT'S ALL ABOUT CHARACTER

1. C. Miller, *The Character Gap: How Good Are We?*, Oxford University Press, 2017.

2. K. Dahlsgaard, C. Peterson, and M. E. P. Seligman, "Shared virtue: the convergence of valued human strengths across culture and history," *Review of General Psychology* 9(3):203–213, 2005.

3. Quoted in *The Character Gap*, 16.

4. *The Character Gap*, chapter 3.

5. L. M. Karakashian, M. I. Walter, A. N. Christopher, and T. Lucas, "Fear of negative evaluation affects helping behavior: the bystander effect revisited," *North American Journal of Psychology* 8(1):13–32, 2006.

6. *The Character Gap*, chapter 7.

7. *The Character Gap*, 135.

8. *The Character Gap*, chapter 8.

9. Epictetus, *Enchiridion*, 33.12–13.

10. Seneca, *Letters to Lucilius*, 11.10.

11. *The Character Gap*, chapter 9.

12. *Letters to Lucilius*, 59.3.

13. *Enchiridion* 33.6.

14. *The Character Gap*, chapter 9; M. van Bommel, J.-W. van Prooijen, H. Elffers, and P. A. M. Van Lange, "Be aware to care: Public self-awareness leads to a reversal of the bystander effect," *Journal of Experimental Social Psychology* 48(4):926–930, 2012.

15. Epictetus, *Discourses*, IV.3.4–5.

16. John Sellars, *The Art of Living: The Stoics on the Nature and Function of Philosophy*, Bristol Classical Press, 2009, 167.

17. Diogenes Laertius, *Lives of the Eminent Philosophers*, translated by Pamela Mensch, Oxford University Press, 2018, 7.39–40.

18. *Lives of the Eminent Philosophers*, 7.3.

19. Epictetus, *Discourses*, I.26.3.

20. Ignatius of Loyola, *Exercitia Spiritualia*, Annotationes 1, Paulist Press, 1991.

21. Musonius Rufus, Fragment 6, *Lectures and Sayings*, translated by Cynthia King, CreateSpace, 2011.

22. Quoted in John Sellars, "Stoic practical philosophy in the imperial period," *Bulletin of the Institute of Classical Studies* 50(94P1), 115–141, June 1, 2007.

23. Epictetus, *Enchiridion*, 10.

24. Marcus Aurelius, *Meditations*, 5.16.

25. Epictetus, *Discourses*, III.21.1–4.

26. Seneca, *Letters to Lucilius*, 2.2–4.

27. Here is a way to find fellow travelers in your philosophical practice: https://stoicfellowship.com.

28. Seneca, *On the Shortness of Life*, 3.

INDEX

© Amy Quint

Massimo Pigliucci is the K. D. Irani Professor of Philosophy at the City College of New York. He holds PhDs in genetics, evolutionary biology, and philosophy. The author or editor of sixteen books, he has published articles in the *New York Times*, the *Wall Street Journal*, the *Washington Post*, and *Salon*, among others. He lives in Brooklyn, New York.